SLOW COOK IT

SLOW COOK IT

Slow-Cooked Meals Packed with Flavor

STERLING EPICURE
New York

STERLING EPICURE
New York

An Imprint of Sterling Publishing
1166 Avenue of the Americas
New York, NY 10036

STERLING EPICURE is a trademark of Sterling Publishing Co., Inc. The distinctive Sterling logo is a registered trademark of Sterling Publishing Co., Inc.

First published in the United Kingdom in 2013 by Pavilion Books Company Limited

First Sterling edition published in 2015

ISBN 978-1-4549-1773-1

Distributed in Canada by Sterling Publishing c/o Canadian Manda Group, 664 Annette Street Toronto, Ontario, Canada M6S 2C8

For information about custom editions, special sales, and premium and corporate purchases, please contact Sterling Special Sales at 800-805-5489 or specialsales@sterlingpublishing.com.

Manufactured in China

2 4 6 8 10 9 7 5 3 1

www.sterlingpublishing.com

NOTES

Ovens and broilers must be preheated to the specified temperature.

Large eggs should be used except where otherwise specified. Free-range eggs are recommended.

Note that some recipes contain raw or lightly cooked eggs. The young, elderly, pregnant women, and anyone with an immune-deficiency disease should avoid these because of the slight risk of salmonella.

Contents

Slow-Cooker First Courses and Sides

Carrot and Coriander Soup

Slow Cooker Recipe

Prep time: 15 minutes
Cooking time: 15 minutes in pan, then about 4 hours on High, plus cooling

---

3 tbsp. butter

1½ cups trimmed and sliced leeks

3 cups sliced carrots

2 tsp. ground coriander

1 tsp. all-purpose flour

4¼ cups (1 liter) hot vegetable stock (see page 44)

⅔ cup (160ml) light cream

salt and freshly ground black pepper

cilantro leaves, roughly torn, to serve

WITHOUT A SLOW COOKER

Complete steps 1 and 2. In step 3, bring to a boil and leave the soup in the pan. Season with salt and ground black pepper, then reduce the heat, cover the pan, and simmer for about 20 minutes until the vegetables are tender. Complete step 4 to finish the recipe.

1 Melt the butter in a large pan. Stir in the leeks and carrots, then cover the pan and cook over low heat for 7–10 minutes until the vegetables begin to become soft.

2 Stir in the ground coriander and flour and cook, stirring, for 1 minute longer.

3 Add the hot stock and bring to a boil, stirring. Season with salt and ground black pepper, then transfer to the slow cooker, cover, and cook on High for 3–4 hours until the vegetables are tender.

4 Leave the soup to cool a little, then blend in batches in a blender or food processor until smooth. Pour into a clean pan and stir in the cream. Adjust the seasoning and reheat slowly on the stovetop—do not boil. Ladle into warm bowls, scatter with torn cilantro leaves, and serve.

Serves 6

Beet Soup

Slow Cooker Recipe

♨ **Prep time:** 15 minutes
Cooking time: 15 minutes in pan, then about 4 hours on High

---

1 tbsp. olive oil

1 onion, finely chopped

3 cups peeled raw beets cut into ½in. (1cm) cubes

2 cups roughly chopped potatoes

6 cups (1.5 liters) hot vegetable stock (see page 44)

juice of 1 lemon

salt and freshly ground black pepper

To serve

½ cup (125ml) sour cream

mixed vegetable chips (optional)

2 tbsp. snipped fresh chives

---

1 Heat the oil in a large pan. Add the onion and cook, stirring, for 5 minutes, or until soft. Add the beets and potatoes and cook for 5 minutes longer.

2 Add the hot stock and the lemon juice and bring to a boil. Season with salt and ground black pepper, then transfer to the slow cooker, cover, and cook on High for 3–4 hours until the beets are tender.

3 Leave the soup to cool a little, then blend in batches in a blender or food processor until smooth. Pour into a clean pan and reheat slowly on the stovetop. Ladle into warm bowls. Swirl 1 tbsp. sour cream on each portion, scatter with a few chips, if you like, and sprinkle with snipped chives to serve.

WITHOUT A SLOW COOKER

Complete step 1. In step 2, bring to a boil and leave the soup in the pan, then reduce the heat and simmer slowly, half-covered, for 25 minutes. Complete the recipe to serve.

FREEZE AHEAD

To make ahead and freeze, prepare the soup to the end of step 2, then cool half or all the soup, pack, and freeze for up to three months. To use, thaw the soup overnight, then simmer over low heat for 5 minutes.

Serves 8

French Onion Soup

Slow Cooker Recipe

Prep time: 30 minutes
Cooking time: 40 minutes in pan, then about 4 hours on Low

6 tbsp. butter

3½ cups sliced onions

3 garlic cloves, crushed

1 tbsp. all-purpose flour

¾ cup plus 2 tbsp. (200 ml) white wine

4¼ cups (1 liter) hot vegetable stock
  (see page 44)

bouquet garni (1 bay leaf and a few fresh
  thyme and parsley sprigs)

salt and freshly ground black pepper

To serve

1 small baguette, cut into slices ½in.
  (1cm) thick

½ cup grated Gruyère cheese
  or cheddar

WITHOUT A SLOW COOKER

Complete step 1. In step 2, bring
to a boil, then reduce the heat and
simmer slowly, uncovered, for
20–30 minutes. Complete steps
3 and 4 to finish the recipe.

1 Melt the butter in a large pan. Add the onions and cook slowly over very low heat, stirring frequently, until very soft and golden brown—this should take at least 30 minutes. Add the garlic and flour and cook, stirring, for 1 minute.

2 Pour in the wine and let it bubble until it reduces by half. Add the hot stock, the bouquet garni, and seasoning, and bring to a boil. Transfer to the slow cooker, cover, and cook on Low for 3–4 hours until the onions are tender.

3 When ready to serve, turn on the broiler. Lightly toast the baguette slices on both sides. Reheat the soup and adjust the seasoning. Discard the bouquet garni.

4 Divide the soup among four flameproof soup bowls. Float two or three slices of toast on each portion and sprinkle thickly with the grated cheese. Place the bowls under the hot broiler until the cheese melts and turns golden brown. Serve at once.

Serves 4

Leek and Potato Soup

Prep time: 10 minutes
Cooking time: 30 minutes in pan, then about 4 hours on Low, plus cooling

2 tbsp. butter

1 onion, finely chopped

1 garlic clove, crushed

3¼ cups trimmed and chopped leeks

1½ cups sliced Idaho potatoes

4½ cups (1.1 liters) hot vegetable stock (see page 44)

crème fraîche or sour cream and snipped chives to garnish

WITHOUT A SLOW COOKER

Complete step 1. In step 2, bring to a boil, then reduce the heat and simmer for 20 minutes, or until the potatoes are tender. Complete steps 3 and 4 to finish the recipe.

1 Melt the butter in a pan over low heat. Add the onion and cook for 10–15 minutes until soft. Add the garlic and cook for 1 minute longer. Add the leeks and cook for 5–10 minutes until soft. Add the potatoes and toss together with the leeks.

2 Pour in the hot stock and bring to a boil. Transfer the soup to the slow cooker, cover, and cook on Low for 3–4 hours until the potatoes are tender.

3 Leave the soup to cool a little, then blend in batches in a blender or food processor until smooth.

4 Pour the soup into a clean pan and reheat slowly on the stovetop—do not boil. Ladle into warm bowls, garnish with crème fraîche and chives, and serve hot.

Serves 4

Split Pea and Ham Soup

Prep time: 15 minutes, plus overnight soaking
Cooking time: 20 minutes in pan, then about 4 hours on High, plus cooling

2½ cups dried yellow split peas, soaked overnight (see Save Money, opposite)

2 tbsp. butter

1 large onion, finely chopped

⅔ cup roughly chopped smoked bacon slices

1 garlic clove, crushed

7 cups (1.7 liters) ham broth or vegetable stock (see page 44)

1 bouquet garni (1 bay leaf and a few fresh parsley and thyme sprigs)

1 tsp. dried oregano

scant 1 cup chopped cooked ham

salt and freshly ground black pepper

cracked black pepper to serve

1 Drain the soaked split peas and set to one side. Melt the butter in a large pan, add the onion, bacon, and garlic, and cook over low heat for about 10 minutes until the onion is soft.

2 Add the split peas to the pan with the broth or stock. Bring to a boil and use a slotted spoon to remove any scum that comes to the surface. Add the bouquet garni and oregano, then season with salt and ground black pepper. Transfer to the slow cooker, cover and cook on High for 3–4 hours until the peas are very soft.

3 Leave the soup to cool a little, then blend half the soup in a blender or food processor until smooth. Pour all the soup into a clean pan and reheat slowly on the stovetop—do not boil. Add the ham and check the seasoning. Ladle into warm bowls and sprinkle with black pepper to serve.

Serves 6

Perfect Vegetables

Nutritious, mouthwatering, and essential to a healthy diet – vegetables are an ideal addition to slow-cooked dishes.

Stewing

1. Cut the vegetables into large bite-size pieces, no more than about 2in. (5cm) square. Put them into a Dutch oven (for oven cooking) or a heavy-bottomed pan (for stovetop cooking). Add salt and freshly ground black pepper and flavorings, if you like (see Perfect stews, opposite), and mix well.

2. Heat the oven to 350°F (325°F convection oven) if you are cooking in the oven.

3. Pour in enough hot stock to come about three-quarters of the way up the vegetables. Cover the pot with a lid or foil and cook for 30–40 minutes until the vegetables are tender, but not disintegrating. Turn the vegetables once and baste with the juices a few times during cooking.

Perfect stews

- ❏ Any vegetable can be stewed; be careful, however, not to overcook it.
- ❏ Ideal flavorings for stewed vegetables include garlic, shallots, curry powder (or Indian spices), and chili sauce or chopped chilies.
- ❏ Potatoes will thicken the dish a little as they release some of their starch.

Perfect braising

- ❏ Carrots, fennel, leeks, celeriac, celery, and cabbage are all good braised.
- ❏ Leave vegetables whole or cut them into chunks. Shred cabbage, then fry lightly before braising.
- ❏ Place the vegetables in a single layer for cooking.

Braising

1. Prepare the vegetables (see Perfect braising, above). Pack tightly in a single layer in a baking dish. Heat the oven to 350°F (325°F convection oven). Dot the vegetables generously with butter and season with salt.

2. Pour in enough hot stock to come halfway up the vegetables. Cover the dish with a lid or foil and cook in the oven for 30–40 minutes until the vegetables are soft. Baste them with the buttery stock a few times during cooking.

2

Braised Belgian Endive in White Wine

Slow Cooker Recipe

Prep time: 5 minutes
Cooking time: about 3 hours on Low

4 tbsp. butter, softened

6 Belgian endive heads, trimmed

juice of ½ lemon

7 tbsp. white wine

salt and freshly ground black pepper

snipped fresh chives to serve

1 Grease the slow cooker dish with 1 tbsp. of the butter. Toss the Belgian endive in the lemon juice and arrange in the bottom of the dish.

2 Season to taste, add the wine, and spread the remaining butter over the top. Cover and cook on Low for 2–3 hours until soft. Scatter with chives to serve.

WITHOUT A SLOW COOKER

Grease a 7-cup (1.7 liter) baking dish instead of the slow cooker. Complete step 1 and the first part of step 2. Cover with foil and cook in the oven for 1 hour, or until soft. Scatter with chives to serve.

Serves 4

Braised Red Cabbage

Prep time: 10 minutes
Cooking time: about 3 hours on Low

1 red onion, finely chopped

½ red cabbage (weight about 1lb. 2oz./ 500g), shredded

1 cooking apple, peeled, cored, and chopped

2 tbsp. soft light brown sugar

1 cinnamon stick

a pinch of ground cloves

¼ tsp. freshly grated nutmeg

2 tbsp. each red wine vinegar and dry red wine

juice of 1 orange

salt and freshly ground black pepper

1 Put all the ingredients into the slow cooker and stir to mix well. Cover and cook on Low for 2–3 hours.

2 When the cabbage is tender, turn off the slow cooker and discard the cinnamon stick. Serve at once, or leave to cool, then put into a bowl, cover, and chill the cabbage overnight or up to 2 days before reheating.

WITHOUT A SLOW COOKER

Heat 2 tbsp. olive oil in a large heavy-bottomed pan. Add the onion and cook gently for 3–4 minutes to soften. Add the cabbage, sugar, spices, vinegars, and orange juice, and season well. Bring to a boil, then reduce the heat, cover the pan, and simmer for 30 minutes. Add the apples and stir through. Cook for 15 minutes longer, or until the cabbage is tender and nearly all the liquid evaporates. Discard the cinnamon stick before serving.

3 To reheat, put the cabbage into a pan, add 2 tbsp. cold water, and cover with a tight-fitting lid. Bring to a boil, then reduce the heat and simmer for 25 minutes.

Serves 8

Ratatouille

Slow Cooker Recipe

Prep time: 20 minutes
Cooking time: 15 minutes in pan, then about 4 hours on High

4 tbsp. olive oil

2 onions, thinly sliced

1 large garlic clove, crushed

12oz. (350g) small eggplants, thinly sliced

3 cups thinly sliced small zucchini

3 cups skinned, seeded, and roughly chopped tomatoes

1 green and 1 red bell pepper, each seeded and sliced

1 tbsp. freshly chopped basil

2 tsp. freshly chopped thyme

2 tbsp. freshly chopped flat-leaf parsley

2 tbsp. sun-dried tomato paste

salt and freshly ground black pepper

1 Heat the oil in a large pan. Add the onions and garlic and fry slowly for 10 minutes, or until soft and golden.

2 Add the eggplants, zucchini, tomatoes, sliced peppers, herbs, tomato paste, and seasoning, and fry, stirring, for 2–3 minutes.

3 Transfer to the slow cooker, cover, and cook on High for 3–4 hours until all the vegetables are tender. Taste and adjust the seasoning. Serve the ratatouille hot or at room temperature.

WITHOUT A SLOW COOKER

Complete steps 1 and 2. In step 3, leave the mixture in the pan, cover tightly, and simmer for 30 minutes, or until all the vegetables are tender. Uncover toward the end if there is too much liquid. Season and serve hot or cool.

Serves 6

Mushroom and Bean Hotpot

Slow Cooker Recipe

Prep time: 15 minutes
Cooking time: 15 minutes in pan, then about 3 hours on Low

3 tbsp. olive oil

1½lb. (700g) cremini mushrooms, roughly chopped

1 large onion, finely chopped

2 tbsp. all-purpose flour

2 tbsp. mild curry paste

⅔ cup (160ml) dry white wine

14oz (400g) can crushed tomatoes

2 tbsp. sun-dried tomato paste

2 cans (15-oz./425g) mixed beans, drained and rinsed

3 tbsp. freshly chopped cilantro leaves and mint

1 Heat the oil in a large pan over low heat. Add the mushrooms and onion and fry until the onion is soft and dark golden. Stir in the flour and curry paste and cook for 1–2 minutes, then add the wine, tomatoes, tomato paste, and beans.

2 Bring to a boil, stirring, then transfer to the slow cooker, cover, and cook on Low for 2–3 hours.

3 Stir in the mango chutney (see page 80) and chopped herbs, then serve.

WITHOUT A SLOW COOKER

Complete step 1. In step 2, leave the mixture in the pan and bring to a boil, then reduce the heat and simmer for 30 minutes, or until most of the liquid reduces. Complete step 3 to finish the recipe.

Serves 6

Lentils with Red Pepper

Prep time: 10 minutes
Cooking time: 20 minutes in pan, then about 4 hours on High

1 tbsp. olive oil

1 large onion, finely chopped

2 celery stalks, diced

2 carrots, diced

2 bay leaves, torn

1½ cups Puy lentils

2½ cups (600ml) hot vegetable stock (see page 44)

1 marinated red bell pepper from a jar, drained and chopped

2 tbsp. freshly chopped flat-leaf parsley, plus extra to garnish

freshly ground black pepper

1 Heat the oil in a pan. Add the onion and cook over low heat for 15 minutes, or until soft. Add the celery, carrots, and bay leaves, and cook, stirring, for 2 minutes longer.

2 Add the lentils with the hot stock and stir everything together. Transfer to the slow cooker, cover, and cook on High for 3–4 hours.

3 Stir in the red pepper and parsley and season with ground black pepper. Leave to stand for 10 minutes, then garnish with extra parsley and serve as a side dish.

WITHOUT A SLOW COOKER

Complete step 1. In step 2, leave the mixture in the pan, half cover with a lid, and simmer over low heat for 25–30 minutes. Complete step 3 to finish the recipe.

Serves 4

Spiced Bean and Vegetable Stew

Prep time: 15 minutes
Cooking time: 10 minutes in pan, then about 3 hours on Low

Slow Cooker Recipe

3 tbsp. olive oil

2 small onions, sliced

2 garlic cloves, crushed

1 tbsp. sweet paprika

1 small dried red chili, seeded and finely chopped

4 cups cubed sweet potatoes

3 cups peeled and cubed pumpkin

4oz. (125g) okra, trimmed

2 cups (450ml) tomato puree

15oz (425g) can navy or cannellini beans, drained and rinsed

2 cups (500ml) hot vegetable stock (see page 44)

salt and freshly ground black pepper

1 Heat the oil in a large pan over very low heat. Add the onions and garlic and cook for 5 minutes.

2 Stir in the paprika and chili and cook for 2 minutes, then add the sweet potatoes, pumpkin, okra, tomato puree, beans, and hot stock. Season generously with salt and ground black pepper and bring to a boil.

3 Transfer to the slow cooker, cover, and cook on Low for 2–3 hours until the vegetables are tender.

SAVE EFFORT

An easy way to get a differently flavored dish is to use 1 tsp. each ground cumin and ground coriander instead of paprika. Garnish the stew with freshly chopped cilantro.

WITHOUT A SLOW COOKER

Complete the recipe to the end of step 2, but leaving out the beans. Cover the pan and simmer for 20 minutes, or until the vegetables are tender. Add the beans and cook for 3 minutes to warm through. Serve immediately.

Poultry and Game Dishes

Perfect Poultry and Game

Poultry and game birds are available all year round to feast on, however, there are seasonal fluctuations with game birds. Although it is illegal to sell wild birds, you'll still have plenty of choice with farm-raised birds.

Hygiene

☐ Raw poultry and meat contain harmful bacteria that can spread easily to anything they touch.

☐ Always wash your hands, kitchen surfaces, cutting boards, knives, and other equipment before and after handling poultry or meat.

☐ Don't let raw poultry or meat touch other foods.

☐ Always cover raw poultry and meat and store in the bottom of the refrigerator, where they can't touch or drip onto other foods.

Poultry identification photos

1 Duck
2 Guinea fowl
3 Chicken
4 Squab
5 Pheasant

3

4

5

Types of chicken

Corn-fed These chickens are fed on corn, rather than standard chicken feed, and have golden yellow flesh and, often, an improved flavor. They weigh about 4½lb. (2kg).

Broiler-fryer Usually young birds, these chickens are tender and can weigh up to 6lb. (2.7kg).

Boiling These birds are usually about 18 months old and have tougher flesh that is better suited to long, slow cooking, such as stewing, poaching, casseroling, or pot-roasting. They usually weigh 5½–6½lb. (2.5–3kg). Sold whole and in pieces.

Squab Usually four to eight weeks old, they weigh only about 14oz. (400g). Whole squab can be roasted or spatchcocked and broiled, portions can be pan-fried, broiled, braised, and pot-roasted.

How to Cut up a Chicken

You can buy pieces of chicken in a supermarket or from a butcher, but it is more economical to cut it up yourself. Use the wing tips and bones to make stock (see page 44).

1   Using a sharp meat knife with a curved blade, cut out the wishbone (see step 1, page 60) and remove the wings in a single piece. Remove the wing tips.

2   With the tail pointing toward you and breast-side up, pull one leg away from the body and cut through the skin between the leg and breast. Pull the leg down until you crack the joint between the thighbone and rib cage. Cut through that joint, then cut through the remaining leg meat. Repeat on the other side.

3   To remove the breast without any bone, make a cut along the length of the breastbone. Slowly pulling the flesh away from the ribs with the knife, work the blade down between the flesh and ribs of one breast and cut it off neatly. (Always cut in, toward the bone.) Repeat on the other side.

4   To remove the breast with the bone in, make a cut along the full length of the breastbone. Using poultry shears, cut through the breastbone, then cut through the rib cage following the outline of the breast meat. Repeat on the other side. Trim any flaps of skin or fat.

3

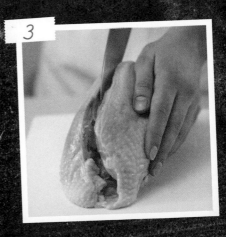

Perfect Casseroling

There are a number of ways to make the most of the delicate taste of poultry. Here's how to make the perfect casserole.

Chicken casserole

To serve 4–6, you will need:
1 chicken boned; 3 tbsp. oil;
1 chopped onion; 2 crushed garlic cloves; 2 chopped celery stalks;
2 chopped carrots; 1 tbsp. all-purpose flour; 2 tbsp. freshly chopped tarragon or thyme; chicken stock and/or wine; salt and freshly ground black pepper

1 Heat the oven to 350°F (325°F convection oven). Cut the chicken legs and breasts in half.

2 Heat the oil in a Dutch oven and brown the chicken all over. Remove the chicken and pour off the excess oil. Add the onion and garlic and brown for a few minutes. Add the vegetables, then stir in the flour and cook for 1 minute. Add the herbs and season. Add the chicken and pour in enough stock and/or wine to come three-quarters of the way up the side of the pan. Bring to a boil, then cover and cook in the oven for 1–1½ hours until the chicken is cooked through and tender.

Braised Garlic Chicken

Prep time: 30 minutes, plus cooling
Cooking time: about 2 hours

2 tbsp. olive oil

1 tbsp. freshly chopped thyme

1½ cups finely chopped cremini
  mushrooms

6 whole chicken legs (drumsticks
  and thighs)

18 thin slices pancetta

2 tbsp. all-purpose flour

2 tbsp. butter

18 small shallots

12 garlic cloves, unpeeled but split

1 bottle (750ml) full-bodied white wine,
  such as Chardonnay

2 bay leaves

salt and freshly ground black pepper

1 Heat the oven to 350°F (325°F
  convection oven). Heat 1 tbsp. of the
  oil in a skillet over medium-high heat.
  Add the thyme and mushrooms and
  fry until all the moisture from the
  mushrooms evaporates. Season with
  salt and ground black pepper, then
  remove from the heat and leave to
  cool.

2 Loosen the skin away from one
  chicken leg and spoon a little of the
  mushroom mixture underneath.
  Season the leg all over with salt and
  pepper, then wrap three pancetta
  slices around the thigh end. Repeat
  with the remaining chicken legs, then
  dust each, using 1 tbsp. of the flour.

3 Melt the butter in a skillet with the
  remaining oil over high heat. Fry the
  chicken legs, in batches, seam-side
  down, until golden. Turn the legs and
  brown the other side—the browning
  should take 8–10 minutes per batch—
  then transfer to a Dutch oven.

4 Put the shallots and garlic into the
  skillet and cook for 10 minutes,
  or until brown. Sprinkle with the
  remaining flour and cook for 1 minute.
  Pour in the wine and bring to a boil,
  stirring. Pour into the pot with the
  chicken and add the bay leaves. Cover
  and cook in the oven for 1½ hours,
  or until the chicken is cooked through
  and tender. Serve hot.

FREEZE AHEAD

To make ahead and freeze, complete the recipe. Cool quickly, then freeze in an airtight container for up to one month. To use, thaw overnight at cool room temperature. Heat the oven to 425°F (400°F convection oven). Put the chicken back into the Dutch oven and reheat in the oven for 15 minutes. Reduce the oven temperature to 350°F (300°F convection oven) and cook for 25 minutes. longer, or until piping hot.

Serves 6

Classic Coq au Vin

Prep time: 15 minutes
Cooking time: about 2¼ hours

1 large chicken, boned (see page 36),
   or 6–8 chicken pieces

2 tbsp. well-seasoned all-purpose flour

7 tbsp. butter

scant 1 cup diced bacon

1 onion, quartered

1 carrot, quartered

4 tbsp. brandy

2½ cups (600ml) dry red wine

1 garlic clove, crushed

1 bouquet garni (2 bay leaves and a few
   fresh parsley and thyme sprigs)

1 tsp. sugar

2 tbsp. vegetable oil

1lb. (450g) pearl onions

a pinch of sugar

1 tsp. wine vinegar

8oz. (225g) button mushrooms

6 slices white bread, crusts removed

salt and freshly ground black pepper

1 Coat the chicken pieces with 1 tbsp.
of the seasoned flour. Melt 2 tbsp. of
the butter in a Dutch oven. Add the
chicken and fry until golden brown
on all sides. Add the bacon, onion
quarters, and carrot, and fry
until soft.

2 Heat the brandy in a small pan, pour
over the chicken, and ignite, shaking
the pot. Pour in the wine and stir
to dislodge any sediment from the
bottom of the Dutch oven. Add the
garlic, bouquet garni, and sugar, and
bring to a boil. Reduce the heat, cover,
and simmer for 1–1½ hours until the
chicken is cooked through.

3 Meanwhile, melt 2 tbsp. of the butter
with 1 tsp. of the oil in a skillet. Add
the button onions and fry until they
begin to brown. Add the sugar and
vinegar together with 1 tbsp. water.
Cover and simmer for 10–15 minutes
until just tender. Keep warm.

4 Melt 2 tbsp. of the butter with 2 tsp.
of the oil in another pan. Add the
button mushrooms and cook for
a few minutes, then turn off the
heat and keep warm. Transfer the
chicken pieces from the Dutch oven

to a deep dish. Surround with the onions and mushrooms and keep hot.

5 Discard the bouquet garni. Skim the excess fat from the cooking liquid, then boil for 3–5 minutes until reduced. Add the remaining oil to the fat in the skillet and fry the bread until golden brown on both sides. Cut each slice into triangles.

6 Work the remaining butter and flour together until evenly blended. Take the Dutch oven off the heat and add small amounts of the blended mixture to the liquid. Stir until smooth, then put back on the stovetop and bring just to a boil. The sauce should be thick and shiny. Take off the heat and season. Put the chicken, onions, and mushrooms back into the Dutch oven and stir. Serve with the fried bread.

Serves 6

Chicken and Potato Casserole

Prep time: 15 minutes
Cooking time: about 2½ hours

2 tbsp. butter, plus a little extra

1 tbsp. vegetable oil

4 chicken quarters, halved

scant 1 cup chopped Canadian bacon

2½lb. (1.2kg) Idaho or other baking
  potatoes, cut into ¼in. (0.5cm) slices

2 large onions, sliced

2 tsp. freshly chopped thyme or ½ tsp.
  dried thyme

2½ cups (600ml) hot chicken stock
  (see page 44)

salt and freshly ground black pepper

freshly snipped chives to garnish

1 Heat the oven to 300°F (250°F convection oven). Heat half the butter and the oil in a large skillet and fry the chicken and bacon for 5 minutes, or until lightly brown.

2 Layer half the potato slices, then half the onion slices in the bottom of a large Dutch oven. Season well, add the thyme, and dot with half the remaining butter.

3 Add the chicken and bacon, season to taste, and dot with the remaining butter. Cover with the remaining onions and finally a layer of potatoes. Season and dot with a little more butter. Pour the hot stock over the top.

4 Cover and cook in the oven for about 2½ hours until the chicken is tender and the potatoes are cooked, adding a little more hot stock if necessary.

5 Just before serving, sprinkle with snipped chives.

3 Good Stocks

Vegetable Stock

To make 4½ cups (1.1 liters), you will need:

1½ cups roughly chopped onions; 1½ cups roughly chopped celery stalks; 1¾ cups trimmed and roughly chopped leeks; 1½ cups roughly chopped carrots; 2 bay leaves; a few fresh thyme sprigs; 1 small bunch of parsley; 10 black peppercorns; ½ tsp. sea salt

1 Put the onions, celery, leeks, and carrots into a large pan. Add 7 cups (1.7 liters) cold water, the bay leaves, thyme sprigs, parsley, peppercorns, and salt, then bring slowly to a boil and skim the surface.

2 Partially cover the pan, reduce the heat, and simmer for 30 minutes. Check the seasoning. Strain the stock through a fine mesh strainer into a bowl and leave to cool. Cover and keep in the refrigerator for up to three days. Use as required.

Chicken Stock

To make 4½ cups (1.1 liters), you will need:

1½ cups roughly chopped onions; 1 cup trimmed and roughly chopped leeks; 1½ cups roughly chopped celery stalks; 3½lb. (1.6kg) raw chicken bones; 1 bouquet garni (2 bay leaves and a few fresh parsley and thyme sprigs); 1 tsp. black peppercorns; ½ tsp. sea salt

1 Put all the ingredients into a large pan and pour in 3 quarts (3 liters) cold water. Bring slowly to a boil and skim the surface.

2 Partially cover the pan, reduce the heat, and simmer slowly for 2 hours. Check the seasoning.

3 Strain the stock through a fine mesh strainer into a bowl and cool quickly. Cover and keep in the refrigerator for up to three days. Remove the solidified fat and use the stock as required.

Giblet Stock

To make 5¼ cups (1.25 liters), you
will need:
turkey giblets; 1 quartered onion;
1 halved carrot; 1 halved celery stalk;
6 black peppercorns; 1 bay leaf

1   Put the giblets into a large pan,
    add the onion, carrot, celery,
    peppercorns, and bay leaf and
    pour in 6¾ cups (1.6 litres) cold
    water. Cover and bring to a boil.
2   Reduce the heat and simmer for
    30 minutes–1 hour, skimming
    occasionally. Strain through
    a strainer. Cool quickly, put into
    a sealable container, and chill for
    up to three days.

Chicken and Pork Terrine

Prep time: 30 minutes, plus overnight chilling
Cooking time: about 2 hours 10 minutes, plus cooling

1 tbsp. olive oil, plus extra to brush

1 onion, finely chopped

2 tbsp. brandy (optional)

12 smoked bacon slices

2 skinless chicken breast halves, cut into
½in. (1cm) pieces (or use turkey breast
or ground chicken or turkey)

1lb. 2oz. (500g) ground pork

⅓ cup roughly chopped pistachios

⅓ cup dried cranberries

¾ tsp. freshly grated nutmeg

2 fresh thyme sprigs, leaves picked off

salt and freshly ground black pepper

fruit chutney and toast to serve

1 Heat the oil in a skillet and cook the
onion slowly for 10 minutes, or until
soft. Carefully add the brandy, if you
like, and bubble for 30 seconds, then tip
the mixture into a large bowl and leave
to cool.

2 Heat the oven to 350°F (300°F
convection oven). Use about 10 of the
bacon slices to line the inside of a 9 x
5in. (23 x 12.5cm) bread pan, leaving

the excess hanging over the sides. Add
the chopped chicken, pork, pistachios,
cranberries, nutmeg, thyme leaves,
and plenty of seasoning (it needs a
fair amount of salt) to the cool onion
mixture and mix well.

3 Press the mixture into the prepared
bread pan and smooth the surface. Fold
any overhanging bacon over the filling
and cover with the remaining slices.
Press down again to make sure the
surface is smooth. Lightly grease
a small sheet of aluminum foil and
press on top of the pan. Wrap the pan
in a double layer of foil, then put into
a roasting pan. Half-fill the roasting
pan with boiling water and carefully
transfer to the oven.

4 Cook for 1½ hours, or until the terrine
feels solid when pressed. Lift the bread
pan out of the water. Unwrap the outer
layers of foil (leaving the greased foil
layer in place). Carefully pour out any
liquid from the terrine (this will set into
a gel if not done). Leave to cool.

5 Sit the bread pan on a baking sheet and place three cans of tomatoes or beans on top of the terrine, resting on the foil layer. Chill overnight.

6 When ready to serve, heat the oven to 400°F (350°F convection oven). Unmold the terrine onto a baking sheet and lightly brush with oil. Brown in the oven for 20–25 minutes. (If you don't want the terrine browned, leave this step out.) Serve the terrine warm or at room temperature, in slices, with fruit chutney and toast.

SAVE TIME

Prepare the terrine to the end of step 5 up to two days ahead. Remove the weights and chill again. Complete the recipe to serve.

Serves 8

Perfect Turkey

Cooking a turkey can be a daunting prospect, especially since very often it's the centerpiece of a once-a-year meal. With planning and following a few simple steps, however, you can produce a perfectly cooked turkey.

Thawing

Leave a frozen turkey in its bag to thaw at cool room temperature, not in the refrigerator. Remove any giblets as soon as they become loose. Once there are no ice crystals inside the body cavity and the legs are flexible, cover and store in the refrigerator. Cook within 24 hours.

Cleaning the bird

Before stuffing a bird, pull out and discard any loose fat from the neck or cavity with your fingers, then dry the bird well using paper towels.

Preparing the bird

Take the bird out of the refrigerator 45 minutes–1 hour before stuffing and roasting to let it to reach room temperature, then clean it (see right).

Stuffing

Loosely stuff the neck end only. Allow 8oz. (225g) stuffing for each 5lb. (2.3kg) weight of bird, and stuff just before cooking. Secure the neck skin with skewers or cocktail picks, or sew using a trussing needle threaded with fine kitchen string.

Resting

Once the turkey is cooked through, leave it to rest for 20–30 minutes before carving. Transfer from the roasting pan to a plate and cover loosely with foil and a clean dish towel. Resting lets the juices settle back into the meat, leaving it moist and easier to carve.

Cooking

Weigh the bird after stuffing to calculate the cooking time. Coat the turkey with butter and season. Wrap loosely in a "tent" of foil, then cook in an oven heated to 375°F (325°F convection oven). Allow 45 minutes per 2¼lb. (1kg), or 20 minutes per 1lb. (450g), plus 20 minutes (see chart on page 62 for timings). Remove the foil about 1 hour before the end of cooking time to brown the bird. Baste regularly. Test that the turkey is cooked (see page 63); if not, return it to the oven and cook 10 minutes longer and test again.

Clementine and Sage Turkey with Madeira Gravy

Prep time: 30 minutes
Cooking time: about 3 hours 40 minutes, plus resting

12lb. (5.4kg) free-range turkey (keep the giblets for stock, if you like—see page 44. Buy the best quality turkey you can to get the maximum flavor and texture)

3 firm clementines

¾oz. (20g) fresh sage

7 tbsp. butter, softened

about 2½ cups stuffing (see pages 56–9)

3 celery stalks

3 carrots, halved lengthwise

salt and freshly ground black pepper

fried clementine halves and stuffing balls to garnish (optional)

For the Madeira gravy

2 tbsp. all-purpose flour

½ cup (125ml) Madeira wine

1¼ cups (300ml) chicken stock (see page 44)

1 tbsp. honey or red currant jelly, if needed

1 Remove the turkey from the refrigerator 1 hour before you stuff it to let it come to room temperature.

2 Heat the oven to 375°F (325°F convection oven). Finely grate the zest from the clementines into a bowl. Halve the zest-free clementines and put to one side. Next, add 2 tbsp. thinly sliced sage leaves (keep the rest of the bunch to one side) to the bowl with the butter and plenty of seasoning and mix well.

3 Put the turkey, breast-side up, on a board. Use tweezers to pluck any feathers from the skin. Loosen the skin at the neck and use your fingers to ease the skin away from the breast meat, until 3½in. (9cm) is free. Spread most of the butter between the skin and meat. Put the rest to one side.

4 Spoon the cold stuffing into the neck cavity, pushing it down between the skin and breast meat and taking care not to overfill. Neaten the shape. Turn

the turkey on to its breast, pull the neck flap down and over the stuffing and secure the skin with a skewer or cocktail picks. Weigh the turkey and calculate the cooking time, allowing 30–35 minutes per 2¼lb. (1kg).

5 Make a platform in a large roasting pan with celery stalks and carrot halves and sit the turkey on top. Put the clementine halves and remaining sage (stems and all) into the turkey cavity, then rub the remaining flavored butter over the bird's breast. Tie the legs with kitchen string, season all over, and cover loosely with foil.

6 Roast for the calculated time, removing the foil for the last 45 minutes of cooking, and basting at least three times during cooking. If the skin is browning too quickly, cover with foil.

7 To check the turkey is cooked, pierce the thickest part of the thigh with a skewer—the juices should run clear. If there are any traces of pink in the juice, put the bird back into the hot oven for 10 minutes, then check again in the same way. Alternatively, use a meat thermometer—the temperature needs to read 172°F when inserted into the thickest part of the breast.

8 When the turkey is cooked, tip the bird so that the juices run into the pan,

then transfer the turkey to a board (put the pan for the gravy to one side). Cover loosely with foil and clean dish towels to keep the heat in. Leave to rest in a warm place for 30 minutes–1¼ hours.

9 To make the gravy, spoon off most of the fat from the roasting pan (leaving the vegetables in the pan). Put over medium heat and add the flour. Cook, stirring well with a wooden spoon, for 1 minute. Gradually add the Madeira, scraping up all the sticky bits from the bottom of the pan, then leave to bubble for a few minutes. Next, stir in the stock and leave to simmer, stirring occasionally, for 5 minutes. Check the seasoning and add the honey or red currant jelly, if needed. Strain into a warm gravy boat, or into a clean pan to reheat when needed.

10 To serve, unwrap the turkey and transfer to a warm plate. Remove the skewer or cocktail picks, then garnish with the fried clementine halves and stuffing balls, if you like. Serve with the gravy.

Serves 8, with
leftovers (see previous page)

Serves 8, with leftovers
(see recipe next page)

Roast Turkey with Lemon-and-Parsley Butter

Prep time: 25 minutes
Cooking time: about 3½ hours, plus resting

12lb. (5.4kg) free-range turkey (keep the giblets for stock to one side—see page 44. Buy the best quality turkey you can to get the maximum flavor and texture)

1 lemon, zested (put the lemon to one side)

7 tbsp. unsalted butter, soft

2 tbsp. finely chopped fresh flat-leaf parsley

1 quantity uncooked Herbed Bread Stuffing (see page 59)

1 red onion, halved

5 fresh bay leaves (optional)

salt and freshly ground black pepper

fresh bay leaves and extra lemon halves browned (cut side down) in oil to garnish (optional)

1 Remove the turkey from the refrigerator 1 hour before you stuff it to let it come to room temperature.

2 Heat the oven to 375°F (325°F convection oven). Put the lemon zest, butter, parsley, and plenty of seasoning into a small bowl and mix well.

3 Put the turkey, breast-side up, on a board. Use tweezers to pluck any feathers from the skin. Loosen the skin at the neck end and use your fingers to ease the skin slowly away from breast meat, until about 3½in. (9cm) is free. Spread the butter mixture between the skin and meat.

4 Spoon the cold stuffing into the neck cavity, pushing it down between the skin and breast meat and taking care not to overfill. Neaten the shape. Turn the turkey over onto its breast, pull the neck flap down and over the stuffing, and secure the neck skin with a skewer or cocktail picks. Weigh the

turkey and calculate the cooking time, allowing 30–35 minutes per 2¼lb. (1kg).

5 Transfer the turkey to a large roasting pan. Cut the zested lemon in half and squeeze the juice over the bird. Put the juiced halves into the bird's cavity, together with the red onion halves and the bay leaves. Tie the legs together with kitchen string, season the bird all over, and cover loosely with foil.

6 Roast for the calculated time, removing the foil for the last 30 minutes, and basting at least four times during roasting. If the skin is browning too quickly, cover with foil again.

7 To check if the turkey is cooked, pierce the thickest part of the thigh with a skewer—the juices should run clear. If there are any traces of pink in the juice, put the bird back into the oven and cook for 10 minutes longer, then check again. Alternatively, use a meat thermometer —the temperature should be 172°F when inserted into thickest part of the breast.

8 When the turkey is cooked, tip the bird so the juices run into the pan, then transfer the turkey to a board (put the roasting pan for the gravy to one side). Cover the turkey well with foil and clean dish towels to keep the heat in, then leave to rest in a warm place for 30 minutes–1¼ hours.

9 When ready to serve, put on a warm plate or board, remove the string, skewer or cocktail picks, and garnish with bay leaves and lemon, if you like.

Top 5 Stuffings

Some people like moist stuffing, cooked inside the bird, while others prefer the crisper result when the stuffing is cooked in a separate dish—why not do half and half and please everyone? All these stuffings—with the exception of the wild rice stuffing—can be made a day ahead or frozen for up to one month. Thaw overnight in the refrigerator. Cook in a heated oven, or alongside the roast.

Best-Ever Sage and Onion Stuffing

To serve eight, you will need:
1 tbsp. olive oil; 1 very finely chopped large onion; 2 tbsp. finely chopped fresh sage; heaped 7 tbsp. fresh white bread crumbs; 2lb. (900g) pork sausage meat; 1 large egg yolk; salt and freshly ground black pepper

1 Heat the oil in a pan and slowly fry the onion until soft and golden. Stir in the sage and leave to cool.
2 Keep 1 tbsp. bread crumbs to one side, then mix the remainder into the sausage meat with the onion and egg yolk. Season with salt and ground black pepper, then leave to cool. Cover and chill overnight, or freeze.
3 Turn the stuffing out into a baking dish that is suitable to serve from, sprinkle with the reserved fresh bread crumbs, and cook in an oven heated to 350°F (325°F convection oven) for 35–40 minutes until cooked through and golden.

Sausage, Cranberry, and Apple Stuffing

To serve eight, you will need:
4 tbsp. butter; 1 finely chopped onion; 1 crushed garlic clove; 10oz. (275g) pork sausage meat; ½ cup dried cranberries; 2 tbsp. freshly chopped parsley; 1 red dessert apple; salt and freshly ground black pepper.

1 Melt the butter in a pan, add the onion, and cook over medium heat for 5 minutes, or until soft. Add the garlic and cook for 1 minute. Tip into a bowl and leave to cool. Add the sausage meat, cranberries, and parsley, then cover and chill overnight, or freeze.

2 Core and chop the apple and add it to the stuffing. Season with salt and ground black pepper and stir well.

3 Turn the stuffing into a baking dish that is suitable to serve from and cook in an oven heated to 400°F (350°F convection oven) for 30 minutes, or until the sausage meat is cooked through.

Fennel and Pine Nut Stuffing

To serve eight, you will need:
6 tbsp. butter, plus extra for greasing; 1 bunch of scallions, sliced; 3 cups roughly chopped fennel; 4 tbsp. freshly chopped tarragon; 4 tbsp. pine nuts, toasted; 5oz. (150g) goat cheese; 2½ cups fresh bread crumbs; 2 large eggs, beaten; grated zest and juice of 1 lemon; salt and freshly ground black pepper

1 Melt the butter in a pan, add the scallions, and cook for 3 minutes. Add the fennel and cook for 5 minutes, then leave to cool.

2 Add the tarragon, pine nuts, cheese, bread crumbs, eggs, and lemon zest and juice. Season with salt and ground black pepper and mix well. Cover and chill in the refrigerator overnight, or freeze.

3 Turn the stuffing into a buttered baking dish and cook in an oven heated to 400°F (350°F convection oven) for 30–40 minutes until golden.

Wild Rice and Cranberry Stuffing

This stuffing is great with goose. If you have the goose giblets, use the liver for this recipe.

To serve six to eight, you will need: heaped ½ cup wild rice; 8oz. (225g) bacon slices, cut into short strips; 1½ cups finely chopped red onions; ½ cup dried cranberries; 1 large egg, beaten; salt and freshly ground black pepper; butter to grease

1   Put the rice into a pan and cover with 3¾ cups (900ml) cold water. Add ¼ tsp. salt and bring to a boil. Reduce the heat and simmer, partly covered, for 45 minutes, or until the rice is tender. Drain and leave to cool.

2   Heat a large skillet, add the bacon, and dry-fry, turning from time to time, until light brown. Remove the bacon with a slotted spoon and transfer to a bowl. (If you have the goose liver, cook it in the same pan for 2–3 minutes, then leave to cool, chop it finely, and add it to the bacon.) Add the onions to the skillet and cook over low heat until soft and translucent. Add the cranberries and cook for 1–2 minutes, then add the mixture to the bacon and leave to cool completely.

3   Add the cooked rice and the egg to the bacon mixture. Season with salt and ground black pepper, then stir thoroughly to combine. Cover and chill overnight.

4   Wrap the stuffing in a buttered piece of aluminum foil and cook in an oven heated to 400°F (350°F convection oven) for 30–40 minutes.

Herbed Bread Stuffing

To serve eight, you will need:
6 tbsp. butter, plus extra to dot;
1 finely chopped onion; 2½ cups fresh
white bread crumbs; 1 tbsp. Italian
herbs; 2 cups (450ml) vegetable
stock; 8 tbsp. finely chopped fresh
mixed herbs, such as parsley, thyme,
sage, and mint, plus extra
to garnish; 2 finely chopped celery
stalks; 2 Braeburn apples, skin on,
cored and finely diced; 1 tbsp. toasted
and chopped hazelnuts; 4 smoked
bacon slices (optional); salt and
freshly ground black pepper

SAVE EFFORT

Prepare the stuffing to the end of step
2 up to 5 hours ahead. Put the
1lb. 2oz. (500g) for the turkey to one
side. With the remaining stuffing,
either complete the recipe to the end
of step 3, then cover and chill, or form
into balls, wrap in bacon slices, and
put on a baking sheet. Cover and
chill. Complete step 4 to serve.

1 Melt the butter in a large skillet,
   add the onion, and cook slowly for
   10 minutes, or until soft. Stir in the
   bread crumbs and mix to combine.
   Next, add the Italian herbs and
   pour in the stock.

2 Mix in the fresh herbs, celery,
   apples, and hazelnuts, and check
   the seasoning. (Don't stir too
   much or the stuffing can become
   gluey). Put 1lb. 2oz. (500g) of the
   stuffing for the turkey to one side.

3 Spoon the remaining stuffing into
   a baking dish suitable to serve
   from (add extra stock if you like
   your stuffing looser) and dot with
   butter. Lay the bacon slices on top,
   if you like.

4 Cook in an oven heated to 375°F
   (325°F convection oven) for 30
   minutes, or until the bacon is crisp
   and the stuffing is piping hot.
   Garnish with extra chopped herbs.

Perfect Roasting

To calculate the roasting time for the chicken see the chart on page 62. Test if it is cooked through at the end of the calulated time by piercing the flesh with a skewer—the juices should be clear.

Trussing

It is not necessary to truss poultry before roasting it, but it gives the bird a neater shape for serving at the table.

1   To remove the wishbone, pull back the flap of skin at the neck end and locate the tip of the bone with a small sharp knife. Run the knife along the inside of the bone on both sides, then on the outside. Take care not to cut deep into the breast meat. Using poultry shears or sharp-pointed scissors, snip the tip of the bone from the breastbone and pull the bone away from the breast. Snip the two ends or pull them out by hand.

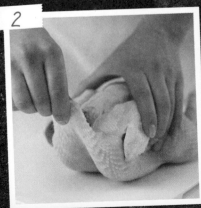

2 Put the wing tips under the breast and fold the neck flap onto the back of the bird. Thread a trussing needle with fine kitchen string and use it to secure the neck flap.

3 Push a metal skewer through both legs, at the joint between the thigh and drumstick. Twist some string around both ends of the skewer and pull firmly to tighten.

4 Turn the bird over. Bring the string over the ends of the drumsticks, pull tight, and tie to secure the legs.

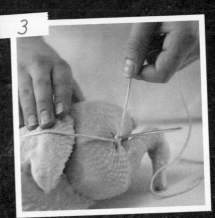

POULTRY AND GAME QUANTITIES FOR ROASTING

	SERVES
Chicken (4½lb./2kg)	about 5
Duck	allow 1lb. (450g) per person
Goose (10lb./4.5kg)	6–8
Grouse	allow 1 bird per person
Guinea fowl	1 bird will serve 2–4
Partridge	allow 1 bird per person
Pheasant	1 bird will serve 2–3
Pigeon	allow 1 bird per person
Quail	allow 2 birds per person
Squab	allow 1 bird per person
Turkey (7¾lb./3.5kg)	10
Woodcock	allow 1 bird per person

Poultry and game roasting times

CHICKEN

To calculate the roasting time for a chicken, weigh the oven-ready bird (including stuffing, if using) and allow 20 minutes per 1lb. (450g) plus 20 minutes extra, in an oven heated to 400°F (350°F convection oven).

OVEN-READY WEIGHT	SERVES	COOKING TIME (APPROX.)
3–3½lb. (1.4–1.6 kg)	4–6	1–1½ hours
4–5lb. (1.8–2.3kg)	6–8	1 hour 50 minutes
5½–6lb. (2.5–2.7kg)	8–10	2¼ hours

TURKEY

To calculate the roasting time for a turkey, weigh the oven-ready bird (including stuffing, if using) and allow 30–35 minutes per 2¼lb. (1kg), or 20 minutes per 1lb. (450g), plus 20 minutes extra, in an oven heated to 375°F (325°F convection oven). Remove the foil about 1 hour before the end of cooking time to brown the bird. Baste regularly during the roasting.

OVEN-READY WEIGHT (at room temperature)	SERVES (APPROX.)	THAWING TIME	COOKING TIME (foil-wrapped)
5–8lb. (2.3–3.6kg)	4–8	15–18 hours	2–3 hours
8–11lb. (3.6–5kg)	8–11	18–20 hours	3–3¼ hours
11–15lb. (5–6.8kg)	11–15	20–24 hours	3¼–4 hours
15–20lb. (6.8–9kg)	15–20	24–30 hours	4–5½ hours

OTHER POULTRY

These figures are a general guideline and recipes can vary. Heat the oven to 400°F (350°F convection oven), and have the birds at room temperature before roasting.

	SERVES	COOKING TIME (APPROX.)
Guinea fowl 3lb. (1.4kg)	3–4	20 minutes per 1lb. (450g)
Duck 4–5½lb. (1.8–2.5kg)	2–4	1½–2 hours
Goose, small 8–12lb. (3.6–5.4kg)	4–7	20 minutes per 1lb. (450g)
Goose, medium 12–14lb. (5.4–6.3kg)	8–11	25 minutes per 1lb. (450g)
Squab	1–2	20 minutes per 1lb. (450g)

How to tell if poultry is cooked through

To check if chicken or turkey is cooked, pierce the thickest part of the meat—usually the thigh—with a skewer. The juices that run out should be golden and clear with no traces of pink; if they're not, put the bird back into the oven and check at regular intervals.

Duck and game birds are traditionally served with the meat slightly pink: if overcooked, the meat may be dry.

Basting

Chicken, turkey and other poultry needs to be basted regularly during roasting to keep the flesh moist. Use an oven mitt to steady the roasting pan and spoon the juices and melted fat over the top of the bird. Alternatively, use a bulb baster.

Resting times

Turkey and goose	up to 1¼ hours
Chicken and duck	15 minutes
Grouse and small game birds	10 minutes

Carving poultry

After resting, put the bird
on a carving board.

1 Steady the bird with a carving
   fork. To cut breast meat, start
   at the neck end and cut slices
   about ¼in. (0.5cm) thick. Use the
   carving knife and fork to lift them
   onto a warm serving plate.
2 To cut off the legs, cut the skin
   between the thigh and breast.
3 Pull the leg down to expose the
   joint between the thigh bone and
   rib cage and cut through that joint.
4 Cut through the joint between the
   thigh and drumstick.
5 To carve meat from the leg (for
   turkeys and very large chickens),
   remove the leg from the carcass
   and joint the two parts of the leg,
   as shown in photo 4. Holding the
   drumstick by the thin end, stand
   it up on the carving board and
   carve slices roughly parallel with
   the bone. The thigh can be carved
   either flat on the board or upright.

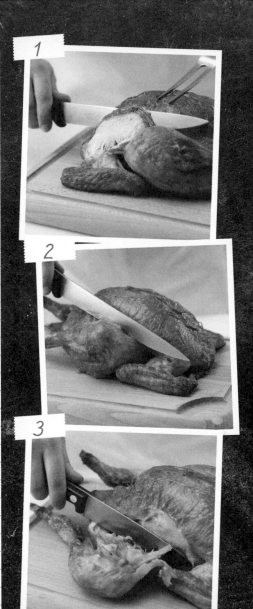

Squab and small game birds

Squab and other small birds, such as grouse, can serve one or two people. To serve two, you will need to split them. The easiest way to do this is with poultry shears while using a carving fork to steady the bird. Insert the shears between the legs and cut through the breastbone. As you do this the bird will open out, exposing the backbone; cut through the backbone.

Storing leftovers

Don't forget the leftovers when the meal is finished—never leave poultry standing in a warm room. Cool quickly in a cold place, then cover and chill.

Guinea Fowl with Fruit

Prep time: 40 minutes, plus marinating
Cooking time: about 25 minutes in pan, then about 6 hours on Low

1½ cups roughly chopped onion

⅔ cup chopped carrot

⅔ cup chopped celery

6–8 guinea fowl pieces (total weight about 4½lb./2kg)

3¼ cups (750ml) red wine

1 tsp. black peppercorns, crushed

1 tbsp. freshly chopped thyme

2 bay leaves

1 cup ready-to-eat prunes

3 tbsp. vegetable oil

8oz. (225g) bacon slices, cut into strips

3 garlic cloves, crushed

1 tsp. harissa paste

1 tbsp. tomato paste

2 tbsp. all-purpose flour

1¼ cups (300ml) chicken stock (see page 44)

2 apples

salt and freshly ground black pepper

mashed potatoes to serve

1 Put the onion, carrot, celery, guinea fowl, 2½ cups (600ml) of the wine, the peppercorns, thyme, and bay leaves into a large bowl. Cover, chill, and leave to marinate for at least 3–4 hours. Soak the prunes in the remaining wine for 3–4 hours.

2 Drain and dry the guinea fowl pieces with paper towels. (Put the vegetables and wine to one side.) Heat 2 tbsp. of the oil in a large skillet. Brown the pieces in batches, if necessary, over medium heat, then transfer them to the slow cooker.

3 Add the marinated vegetables and the bacon to the skillet (keep the marinade to one side) and stir-fry for 5 minutes. Add the garlic, harissa, and tomato paste, and cook for 1 minute. Mix in the flour and stir for 1 minute. Add the reserved marinade and stock, and bring to a boil, stirring, then pour into the slow cooker and season well. Cover and cook on Low for 4–6 hours until the guinea fowl is cooked through.

4 Heat the remaining oil in a pan. Core the apples and cut into wedges, then cook for 2–3 minutes on each side until golden. Put to one side.

5 Remove the guinea fowl pieces from the slow cooker. Strain the sauce and put back into the slow cooker with the guinea fowl. Add the prunes and any juices and the apple. Leave to stand for 10 minutes. Serve hot with mashed potatoes.

WITHOUT A SLOW COOKER

Complete step 1. Use a Dutch oven instead of the slow cooker. In step 2, put the pieces to one side after browning, then continue with step 3 until you add the liquid. Bring to a boil, then season, cover, and cook in an oven heated to 325° F (300°F convection oven) for 40 minutes. Complete steps 4 and 5, returning the sauce to the Dutch oven. Reheat in the oven for 10 minutes before serving.

Serves 6

Goose with Roasted Apples

Prep time: 30 minutes
Cooking time: 3 hours, plus resting

6 small red onions, halved

7 small red dessert apples, halved

11lb. (5kg) oven-ready goose, patted dry
and seasoned inside and out

1 small bunch of fresh sage

1 small bunch of fresh rosemary

1 bay leaf

salt and freshly ground black pepper

For the gravy

1 tbsp. all-purpose flour

1¼ cups (300ml) red wine

¾ cup plus 2 tbsp. (200ml) giblet stock
(see page 45)

1 Heat the oven to 450°F (400°F convection oven). Put half an onion and half an apple inside the goose with half the sage and rosemary and the bay leaf. Tie the legs together with string. Push a long skewer through the wings to tuck them in. Put the goose, breast-side up, on a rack in a roasting pan. Prick the breast all over and season with salt and ground black pepper. Put the remaining onions around the bird, then cover loosely with aluminum foil.

2 Roast in the oven for 30 minutes, then take the pan out of the oven and baste the goose with the fat that has run off. Remove and put any excess fat to one side. Reduce the oven temperature to 375°F (325°F convection oven) and roast for 1½ hours longer, removing any excess fat every 20–30 minutes.

3 Remove the foil from the goose. Remove excess fat from the pan, then add the remaining apples. Sprinkle the goose with the remaining herbs and roast for 1 hour longer, or until cooked through. To test if the bird is cooked, pierce the thickest part of the thigh with a skewer—the juices should run clear. If there are any traces of pink in the juice, put the bird back into the oven and roast for 10 minutes, then check again in the same way. Alternatively, use a meat thermometer—the temperature needs

to read 172°F when inserted into the thickest part of the breast.

4 Take the goose out of the oven and put it on a warm serving plate. Cover with foil and leave to rest for 30 minutes. Remove the apples and onions and keep warm.

5 To make the gravy, pour out all but 1 tbsp. of the fat from the roasting pan, then stir in the flour, add the wine and stock, and bring to a boil. Cook, stirring, for 5 minutes.

6 Carve the goose, cut the roast apples into wedges, and serve with the goose, onions and gravy.

Serves 6–8

Pork and Ham Dishes

Great Big Pork Pie

Prep time: 30 minutes, plus overnight chilling
Cooking time: about 1 hour 20 minutes, plus cooling

For the pastry dough

vegetable oil to grease

4⅔ cups cups all-purpose flour, plus
  extra to dust

1 tsp. salt

1 cup plus 2 tbsp. lard

For the filling

1½ tsp. vegetable oil

1 onion, finely chopped

2¼lb. (1kg) ground pork

6 smoked bacon slices, cut into ½in.
  (1cm) pieces

¼ tsp. apple pie spice

a small handful of fresh parsley,
  finely chopped

½ tsp. salt

4 tbsp. onion jam or caramelized onions

1 large egg, beaten

7 tbsp. chicken stock (see page 44)

1 sheet leaf gelatin

freshly ground black pepper

1 Grease an 8in. (20cm) springform
  cake pan with oil and put on a large
  baking sheet. To make the dough,
  put the flour and salt into a food
  processor. Next, melt the lard with 1¼
  cups (300ml) water in a small pan and
  bring to a boil. With the motor of the
  processor running, add the hot lard
  mixture and blend until the dough
  nearly comes together. Tip onto
  a work surface, bring together with
  your hands, and knead until smooth.

2 Break off two-thirds of the dough (put
  the remaining one-third to one side,
  uncovered) and roll out on a lightly
  floured surface until about ½in. (1cm)
  thick. Use to line the prepared pan,
  leaving some dough hanging over the
  side. Chill for 10 minutes. Cover the
  remaining dough and put to one side
  at room temperature.

3 Heat the oven to 350°F (325°F
  convection oven). To make the filling,
  heat the oil in a small skillet and
  slowly cook the onion for 8 minutes,

or until soft. Tip into a large bowl and leave to cool for a couple of minutes, then mix in the ground pork, bacon, apple pie spice, parsley, ½ tsp. salt, and lots of ground black pepper.

4 Tip half the filling into the chilled, lined pan and pat down firmly. Spread the onion jam or caramelized onions over the filling and top with the remaining filling, pressing down as before.

5 Roll out the remaining dough as before until large enough to cover the pie. Place on top of the filling, then trim and crimp the edge. (Make sure the crimped edge sits inside the perimeter of the pan or the pie will be hard to remove.) Brush the top with some of the beaten egg—don't brush the outer edge of the crimping, or the dough will stick to the pan.

6 Bake for 40 minutes, then carefully unclip and remove the outside ring of the pan, leaving the pie on its base on the baking sheet. Brush all over with egg and put back into the oven for 30–35 minutes to set the sides and finish cooking through. Take out of the oven.

7 Pour the cold stock into a pan and add the gelatin leaf. Leave to soak for 5 minutes, then heat slowly until it dissolves. Pour into a measuring jug.

8 Filling the pie with the stock mixture isn't an essential step, but there'll be a gap between the meat and pastry if you don't. Use the tip of a knife or a skewer to poke a small hole in the top of the pie. Using a fine funnel (or a steady hand), pour a little stock into the hole and wait for it to be absorbed. Keep adding stock gradually until the pie will take no more. Leave the pie to cool for 30 minutes, then chill overnight. Leave to come to room temperature before serving.

Cuts into 12 slices

Veal and Ham Pie

Prep time: 45 minutes, plus chilling
Cooking time: about 3½ hours, plus cooling

3 or 4 small veal bones

1 small onion

1 bay leaf

4 black peppercorns

4⅔ cups diced boneless veal

1½ cups diced cooked ham

1 tbsp. freshly chopped flat-leaf parsley

grated zest and juice of 1 lemon

1 tbsp. salt

½ tsp. ground black pepper

⅔ cup (160ml) milk and ⅔ cup (160ml) water mixed

⅔ cup lard

3 cups all-purpose flour, plus extra to dust

1 large egg, hard-boiled

1 large egg, beaten

1 Put the bones, onion, bay leaf, and peppercorns into a pan and cover with water. Simmer for 20 minutes, then boil to reduce the liquid to ⅔ cup (160ml). Strain, cool, and chill until needed. Line the bottom of an 8in. (20cm) springform cake pan.

2 Mix together the diced veal, diced ham, parsley, lemon zest and juice, 1 tsp. of the salt, and the pepper.

3 Bring the milk and water and the lard to a boil in a pan, then gradually beat it into the flour and remaining salt in a bowl. Knead for 3–4 minutes.

4 Roll out two-thirds of the dough on a lightly floured surface and mold it into the springform cake pan. Cover and chill for 30 minutes. Keep the remaining dough covered. Heat the oven to 425°F (400°F convection oven).

5 Spoon half the meat mixture and 2 tbsp. of the chilled gelled stock from step 1 into the lined pan. Put the hard-boiled egg in the middle and cover with the remaining meat mixture and 2 more tbsp. of the stock. Roll out the remaining dough to make a lid, then place on top of the meat mixture, sealing the dough edges well. Decorate with remaining dough and make a small steam hole in the middle. Glaze with the beaten egg.

6 Bake for 30 minutes. Cover loosely with foil, reduce the oven temperature to 350°F (325°F convection oven) and bake for 2½ hours longer. Cool on a wire rack.

7 Warm the remaining gelled stock until liquid, then pour into the hole in the middle of the pie. Leave the pie to cool again, then chill the pie until ready to unmold and serve.

FREEZE AHEAD

To make ahead and freeze, complete the recipe and cool completely, then freeze the pie whole, or sliced, wrapped in plastic wrap for up to one month. (Wrapped slices can be stacked on top of each other.) To serve, thaw in the refrigerator or at cool room temperature.

Cuts into 12 slices

Spicy Pork and Bean Stew

Prep time: 15 minutes

Cooking time: about 30 minutes in pan, then about 4 hours on Low

3 tbsp. olive oil

14oz. (400g) pork tenderloin, cubed

1 red onion, sliced

2 leeks, trimmed and cut into chunks

2 celery stalks, trimmed and cut
    into chunks

1½ tsp. harissa paste

1 tbsp. tomato paste

15oz. (425g) can cherry tomatoes

⅔ cup (160ml) hot vegetable or chicken
    stock (see page 44)

15oz. (425g) can navy or cannellini
    beans, drained and rinsed

1 marinated red bell pepper in oil,
    drained and sliced

salt and freshly ground black pepper

freshly chopped flat-leaf parsley
    to garnish

Greek yogurt, lemon wedges, and crusty
    bread to serve

1 Heat 2 tbsp. of the oil in a large skillet.
   Add the pork and fry in batches until
   brown. Transfer to the slow cooker.

2 Heat the remaining oil in the
   skillet. Add the onion and fry for
   5–10 minutes until soft. Add the leeks
   and celery and cook for 5 minutes.
   Add the harissa and tomato paste and
   cook for 1–2 minutes, stirring all the
   time. Add the tomatoes and hot stock
   and season well. Bring to a boil, then
   pour into the slow cooker, cover, and
   cook on Low for 3–4 hours.

3 Stir in the drained beans and red
   bell pepper and leave to stand for
   5 minutes to warm them through.
   Garnish with parsley and serve with
   a dollop of yogurt, a grinding of black
   pepper, lemon wedges for squeezing
   over, and chunks of crusty bread.

Complete steps 1 and 2, but fry the pork in a Dutch oven. In step 2, bring to a boil, then transfer the covered pot to the oven and cook for 25 minutes. Complete step 3 to finish the recipe.

For an easy way to get a brand new dish, replace the pork with the same quantity of lean lamb, such as leg, trimmed of excess fat and then cut into bite-size cubes.

Serves 4

Perfect Ham

Hams come in different sizes and cures, some fresh and others smoked or cured. Some cures are very salty, making it necessary to soak the ham before cooking, so check with your butcher or read the label carefully.

Preparing and cooking ham

1 If the ham needs to be soaked, place it in a large container that will hold it comfortably with plenty of space for water. Pour cold water over the ham to cover and weigh it down if necessary. Leave to soak overnight, then drain well.

2 Put the ham into a large Dutch oven and cover with fresh cold water. Add a few sprigs of parsley, a few peppercorns, a bay leaf, and a chopped onion to the water, if you like. Bring to just below boiling point—do not let the water boil or the meat will be tough. Skim off any surface scum. Simmer for 25 minutes per 1lb. (450g), checking occasionally to make sure it is completely covered with water, topping up, if necessary.

3 Leave the ham to cool in the water, then transfer to a roasting pan. (Save the broth for soup making.)

4 Heat the oven to 400°F (350°F convection oven). Remove the rind and neatly trim the fat so there is an ¼–½in. (0.5–1cm) layer left on the meat.

5 Score the fat with parallel lines about 2in. (5cm) apart, then score on the diagonal to make diamond shapes. Press a clove into the middle of each diamond.

6 Spread prepared mustard thinly and evenly over the ham —or glaze as the recipe suggests. Sprinkle with soft brown sugar to make a light but even coating. Bake the ham for 30 minutes, or until golden brown.

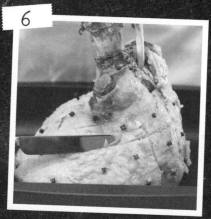

Ginger-and-Honey-Glazed Ham

Prep time: about 30 minutes
Cooking time: 5¾ hours

10–15lb. (4.5–6.8kg) unsmoked fresh
   ham roast on the bone

2 shallots, halved

6 cloves

3 bay leaves

2 celery stalks, cut into 2in. (5cm) pieces

2 tbsp. prepared mustard

2in. (5cm) piece of ginger root, peeled
   and thinly sliced

For the glaze

packed 1 cup dark brown sugar

2 tbsp. honey

8 tbsp. brandy or Madeira

For the chutney

4 mangoes, peeled, sliced, and chopped
   into 2in. (5cm) chunks

1 tsp. apple pie spice

4 cardamom pods, seeds removed and
   crushed

½ tsp. ground cinnamon

4 tbsp. raisins

1 Put the ham into a large pan. Add the shallots, cloves, bay leaves, celery, and enough cold water to cover. Bring to just below a boil, then cover, reduce the heat, and simmer slowly for about 5 hours. Remove any scum with a slotted spoon. Lift the ham out of the pan, discard the vegetables and herbs, and leave to cool.

2 Heat the oven to 400°F (350°F convection oven). Using a sharp knife, carefully cut away the ham's thick skin to leave an even, thin layer of fat. Score a diamond pattern in the fat and put the ham into a roasting pan. Smother evenly with the mustard and tuck the ginger into the scored fat.

3 To make the glaze, put the sugar, honey, and brandy or Madeira into a pan and heat until the sugar dissolves. Brush over the ham.

4 Mix all the chutney ingredients in a bowl, then add any remaining glaze and spoon around the ham.

5 Cook the ham for 30–40 minutes, basting every 10 minutes. Remove the ham from the roasting pan and put to one side. Stir the chutney and put it under a hot broiler for 5 minutes to let the mango caramelize. Transfer the chutney to a small dish and serve with the ham.

Serves 8–10

Cumberland-Glazed Baked Ham

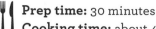

Prep time: 30 minutes
Cooking time: about 4¼ hours

10lb. (4.5kg) smoked fresh ham roast
on the bone

2 celery stalks, roughly chopped

1 onion, quartered

1 carrot, roughly chopped

1 tsp. black peppercorns

1 tbsp. cloves

For the Cumberland glaze

grated zest and juice of ½ lemon and
½ orange

4 tbsp. red currant jelly

1 tsp. Dijon mustard

2 tbsp. port wine

salt and freshly ground black pepper

1 Put the ham into a large Dutch oven.
   Add the celery, onion, carrot, and
   peppercorns. Cover the meat and
   vegetables with cold water and bring
   to a boil, then cover the pot, reduce
   the heat, and simmer for 2¾–3½ hours,
   or allowing 15–20 minutes per 1lb.

(450g) plus 15 minutes. Lift the ham
out of the pan. Heat the oven to 400°F
(350°F convection oven).

2 Meanwhile, make the glaze. Heat the
   lemon and orange zests and juices, red
   currant jelly, mustard, and port wine
   in a pan to dissolve the jelly. Bring
   to a boil and bubble for 5 minutes,
   or until syrupy. Season with salt and
   ground black pepper to taste.

3 Remove the ham rind and score the
   fat in a diamond pattern. Put the ham
   into a large roasting pan, then stud
   the fat with the cloves. Spoon the
   glaze evenly over the roast.

4 Roast the ham for 40 minutes, basting
   the meat with any juices. Add the
   red currant sprigs 10 minutes before
   the end of the cooking time. Serve
   the ham hot or cold, carved into thin
   slices.

Serves 16

Pork and Apple Hotpot

Prep time: 15 minutes
Cooking time: about 2¼ hours

1 tbsp. olive oil

2lb. (900g) pork steaks cut from the shoulder

3 onions, cut into wedges

1 large cooking apple, peeled, cored, and thickly sliced

1 tbsp. all-purpose flour

2½ cups (600ml) hot mild vegetable or chicken stock (see page 44)

¼ Savoy cabbage, sliced

2 fresh thyme sprigs

2lb. (900g) large potatoes, cut into ¾in. (2cm) slices

2 tbsp. butter

salt and freshly ground black pepper

1 Heat the oven to 325°F (300°F convection oven). Heat the oil in a large, nonstick pan with a tight-fitting lid until very hot, then fry the steaks, two at a time, for 5 minutes, or until colored all over. Remove the steaks from the pan and put to one side.

2 In the same pan, fry the onions for 10 minutes, or until soft—add a little water if they start to stick. Stir in the apple and cook for 1 minute, then add the flour to soak up the juices. Gradually add the hot stock and stir until smooth. Season, then stir in the cabbage and add the pork. Throw in the thyme, then overlap the potato slices on top and dot with the butter.

3 Cover tightly and cook near the top of the oven for 1 hour. Remove the lid and cook for 30–45 minutes longer until the potatoes are tender and golden. Put the hotpot under a hot broiler for 2–3 minutes to crisp the potatoes, if you like.

FREEZE AHEAD

If you are going to freeze this dish, then use a Dutch oven or other casserole that is both freezer- and flameproof. Complete the recipe and cool quickly, then freeze in the pot for up to three months. To use, thaw overnight at cool room temperature. Heat the oven to 350°F (325°F convection oven). Pour 4 tbsp. hot stock over the hotpot, then cover and reheat for 30 minutes or until piping hot. Uncover and crisp the potatoes under a hot broiler for 2–3 minutes.

Serves 4

Perfect Roast Pork

Loin of pork produces wonderfully crisp skin, but many other pork roasts are also suitable for roasting, from quick-cooking tenderloin to pork belly, which requires long, slow roasting for melt-in-the-mouth succulence.

Crisp skin and carving

Perfect crisp skin

- ❑ If possible, ask a butcher to score the skin for you.
- ❑ The pork skin needs to be completely dry. Remove all the wrapping and pat the skin dry with paper towels.
- ❑ Leave the roast uncovered in the refrigerator overnight to dry out the skin.
- ❑ If the skin hasn't been scored, use a craft knife, your sharpest knife, or a razor blade to score the skin, cutting about halfway into the fat underneath; don't cut into the meat.
- ❑ Rub the scored skin with a little olive oil and salt.
- ❑ Once cooked, if the skin isn't as crisp as you'd like, you can still rescue it. Remove the skin from the meat and put the whole piece onto a cookie sheet. Broil the pork until crisp and puffed—watch carefully to avoid scorching, and turn the cookie sheet to avoid any hot spots.

Carving pork with crisp skin

1. It is much easier to slice cooked pork if you first remove the crisp skin. Remove any string and position the carving knife just under the skin on the topmost side of the roast. Work the knife under the crisp skin, taking care not to cut into the meat, until you can lift it off with your fingers.

2. Slice the meat, then snap the crisp skin into servings.

Perfect Roast Pork Belly

Prep time: 15 minutes, plus drying
Cooking time: about 3½ hours, plus resting

3lb. 2oz. (1.5kg) piece pork belly

salt

1 Using a small, sharp knife, score lines into the skin, cutting into the fat, about ½in. (1cm) apart, but not so deep that you cut into the meat. Pat the pork completely dry, then leave uncovered at room temperature to air- dry for about 45 minutes.

2 Heat the oven to 425°F (400°F convection oven). Rub lots of salt over the pork skin. Rest a wire rack in a deep roasting pan and put the pork, skin-side up, on the rack. Roast for 30 minutes, then reduce the oven temperature to 325°F (300°F convection oven) and continue roasting for 3 hours longer—by this time the skin should be crisp and golden. If not, don't panic, crisp it up under the broiler— see page 86.

3 Transfer the pork to a board and, using a sharp knife, slice off the crisp skin (about the outer ¾in./2cm). Cover the pork meat loosely with foil and leave to rest for 30–40 minutes.

4 Cut the crisp skin into six long strips, then cut the pork belly into six neat, equal portions. Serve each portion topped with a strip of crisp skin.

Serves 6

Beef and Lamb Dishes

Parson's "Venison"

Prep time: 10 minutes, plus overnight marinating
Cooking time: about 2½ hours, plus cooling

2 tbsp. butter

1 small onion, finely chopped

1½ cups finely chopped mushrooms

scant 1 cup finely chopped cooked ham

2 tbsp. snipped fresh chives

4–4½lb. (1.8–2kg) leg of lamb, boned

salt and freshly ground black pepper

For the marinade

¾ cup plus 2 tbsp. (200ml) dry red wine

5 tbsp. port wine

6 juniper berries, crushed

¼ tsp. ground allspice

3 tbsp. red wine vinegar

1 bay leaf

¼ tsp. freshly grated nutmeg

1 Melt half the butter in a pan. Add the onion and mushrooms and cook, stirring frequently, until the onion is soft but not brown. Stir in the ham and chives and season to taste. Leave to cool.

2 Season the lamb inside and out with ground black pepper, then spread the onion mixture over the inside. Roll up tightly and tie securely. Put the lamb in a large, nonmetallic bowl.

3 Mix all the ingredients for the marinade. Pour over the lamb, cover, and leave in a cool place for 24 hours, turning occasionally.

4 The next day, heat the oven to 350°F (325°F convection oven). Remove the meat from the marinade, drain, and pat dry. Put the marinade to one side. Melt the remaining butter in a Dutch oven. Add the meat and brown on all sides over medium-high heat.

5 Pour in the marinade and bring almost to a boil, then cover and cook in the oven for 1¾–2 hours until the meat is tender, basting occasionally with the marinade.

6 Transfer the meat to a warm plate. Skim the fat from the surface of the liquid, then boil rapidly until syrupy. Remove the bay leaf, adjust the seasoning, and serve with the meat.

Serves 6

Lamb and Orzo Stew

Prep time: 10 minutes
Cooking time: about 2 hours

1 tbsp. vegetable oil

2¼lb. (1kg) diced lamb leg or shoulder, excess fat trimmed

2 red onions, finely sliced

1 tbsp. dried oregano

1 tsp. ground cinnamon

15oz. (425g) can crushed tomatoes

4¾ cups (1.2 liters) vegetable stock (see page 44)

1 cup orzo pasta

⅓ cup roughly chopped pitted black olives

a large handful of fresh parsley, roughly chopped

salt and freshly ground black pepper

1 Heat the oil in a large Dutch oven or flameproof pan with a lid and brown the lamb in batches. Once all the meat is brown, lift out and put to one side on a plate.

2 Put the pot or pan back onto the heat, add the onions, and cook slowly for 10 minutes, or until soft—add a little water if the pan looks too dry. Stir in the oregano and cinnamon, and cook for 1 minute, then stir in the tomatoes, stock, and lamb. Cover and simmer for 1¼ hours, stirring occasionally, or until the lamb is tender.

3 Stir the orzo into the pot or pan and cook, uncovered, for 10–12 minutes longer until the orzo is tender. (Once the orzo is tender, it will continue to swell on standing. If you're not serving it immediately, add a little extra water until the desired consistency is reached.) Next, stir in the olives and most of the parsley. Check the seasoning and garnish with the remaining parsley. Serve immediately.

94

FREEZE AHEAD

To make ahead and freeze, prepare the stew to the end of step 2, then leave to cool completely. Transfer the mixture to a freezer container, cover, and freeze for up to three months.

Leave to thaw overnight in the refrigerator. Reheat slowly in a large pan and complete the recipe.

Serves 6

Lamb and Barley Stew

Prep time: 15 minutes
Cooking time: 2½ hours

2 tbsp. wholewheat flour

3lb. (1.4kg) boned leg or shoulder
of lamb, trimmed of fat and cubed

3 bacon slices

2 tbsp. butter

2 onions, chopped

2 carrots, sliced

1 cup diced turnip or rutabaga

2 celery stalks, diced

2 tbsp. pearl barley

2 tsp. mixed freshly chopped herbs, such
as thyme, rosemary, parsley, basil

1¼ cups (300ml) lamb or beef stock

salt and freshly ground black pepper

freshly chopped flat-leaf parsley
to garnish

1 Season the flour with salt and ground black pepper, then toss the lamb in the flour and shake off the excess.

2 Dry-fry the bacon in a large Dutch oven until the fat runs. Add the butter and lamb and fry until it is brown all over, stirring. Using a slotted spoon, remove the lamb and bacon from the pot and put to one side.

3 Add the onions, carrots, turnip or rutabaga, and the celery to the pot, and fry for 5–10 minutes until all the vegetables are beginning to brown.

4 Put the lamb back into the pot, add the pearl barley and herbs, and pour in the stock. Bring to a boil, then reduce the heat, cover, and simmer for 2 hours, stirring occasionally, or until the lamb is tender.

5 Serve hot, sprinkled with parsley.

Serves 6

Lamb and Leek Hotpot

Prep time: 20 minutes
Cooking time: 2¾ hours

4 tbsp. butter

2¼ cups trimmed and sliced leeks

1 onion, chopped

1 tbsp. olive oil

1¾lb. (800g) cubed lamb shoulder
tossed with 1 tbsp. all-purpose flour

2 garlic cloves, crushed

1¾lb. (1.4kg) waxy potatoes, thinly sliced

3 tbsp. freshly chopped flat-leaf parsley

1 tsp. freshly chopped thyme

1¼ cups (300ml) lamb stock

⅔ cup (160ml) heavy cream

salt and freshly ground black pepper

1 Melt half the butter in a large Dutch oven. Add the leeks and onion and stir to coat, then cover and cook over low heat for 10 minutes. Transfer the leeks and onion to a plate.

2 Heat the oil in the pot. Season the lamb with plenty of salt and black pepper. Add the pieces of lamb and brown in batches, adding the garlic with the last batch. Remove and put to one side on a separate plate.

3 Heat the oven to 325°F (300°F convection oven). Put half the potatoes in a layer over the bottom of the Dutch oven and season. Add the meat, then spoon the leek mixture on top. Arrange a layer of overlapping potatoes on top of that and sprinkle with herbs, then pour in the stock.

4 Bring to a boil on the stovetop, then cover and transfer to a low shelf in the oven and cook for about 1 hour 50 minutes. Take out of the oven, dot with the remaining butter, and pour the cream over the top. Put back into the oven and cook, uncovered, for 30–40 minutes until the potatoes are golden brown.

Serves 6

Irish Stew

1½lb. (700g) boneless middle neck lamb chops, fat trimmed

2 onions, thinly sliced

1lb. (450g) potatoes, thinly sliced

1 tbsp. freshly chopped flat-leaf parsley, plus extra to garnish

1 tbsp. dried thyme

1¼ cups (300ml) hot lamb stock

salt and freshly ground black pepper

1 Heat the oven to 325°F (300°F convection oven). Layer the meat, onions, and potatoes in a Dutch oven, sprinkling some herbs and salt and ground black pepper between each layer. Finish with a layer of potato, overlapping the slices neatly.

2 Pour the hot stock over the potatoes, then cover with a sheet of aluminum foil and the lid. Cook in the oven for about 2 hours until the meat is tender.

3 Turn on the broiler. Uncover the pot and remove the foil. Put under the broiler to brown the top of the potatoes. Sprinkle with chopped parsley and serve immediately.

Serves 4

Braised Oxtails

Prep time: 20 minutes
Cooking time: about 4½ hours

2 oxtails (total weight about 3½lb./1.6kg), trimmed

2 tbsp. all-purpose flour

4 tbsp. vegetable oil

2 large onions, sliced

3¾ cups (900ml) beef stock

⅔ cup (160ml) dry red wine

1 tbsp. tomato paste

finely grated zest of ½ lemon

2 bay leaves

2 carrots, chopped

3 cups chopped parsnips

salt and freshly ground black pepper

freshly chopped flat-leaf parsley to garnish

1 Cut the oxtails into large pieces. Put the flour into a resealable plastic bag and season with salt and ground black pepper, then toss the meat in it. Heat the oil in a large Dutch oven and brown the oxtail pieces, a few at a time. Remove from the pot with a slotted spoon and put to one side.

2 Add the onions to the pot and fry over medium heat for about 10 minutes until soft and light brown. Stir in any remaining flour.

3 Stir in the stock, red wine, tomato paste, lemon zest, and bay leaves, and season with salt and ground black pepper. Bring to a boil, then put the oxtails back into the pot and reduce the heat. Cover and simmer very slowly for 2 hours.

4 Skim off the fat from the surface, then stir in the carrots and parsnips. Recover the pot and simmer very slowly for 2 hours longer, or until the oxtails are very tender.

5 Skim all the fat from the surface, then check the seasoning. Serve scattered with chopped parsley.

Serves 6

Peppered Winter Stew

Prep time: 20 minutes
Cooking time: about 2¾ hours

2 tbsp. all-purpose flour

2lb. (900g) venison, beef, or lamb, cut into 1½in. (4cm) cubes

5 tbsp. vegetable or olive oil

8oz. (225g) whole button onions or shallots

1½ cups finely chopped onions

4 garlic cloves, crushed

2 tbsp. tomato paste

½ cup (125ml) red wine vinegar

1 bottle (750ml) dry red wine

2 tbsp. red currant jelly

1 small bunch of fresh thyme

4 bay leaves

6 cloves

about 6 cups mixed root vegetables, such as carrots, parsnips, turnips, and celeriac, cut into 1½in. (4cm) chunks; carrots cut a little smaller

2½–3¾ cups (600–900ml) beef stock

salt and freshly ground black pepper

1 Heat the oven to 350°F (300°F convection oven). Put the flour into a resealable plastic bag and season with salt and ground black pepper, then toss the meat in it, in batches, if necessary.

2 Heat 3 tbsp. of the oil in a large Dutch oven over medium heat and brown the meat well in small batches. Remove and put to one side.

3 Heat the remaining oil and fry the button onions or shallots for 5 minutes, or until golden. Add the chopped onion and the garlic and cook, stirring, until soft and golden. Add the tomato paste and cook for 2 minutes longer, then add the vinegar and wine and bring to a boil. Bubble for 10 minutes.

4 Add the red currant jelly, thyme, bay leaves, 1 tbsp. coarsely ground black pepper, the cloves, and meat to the pan, along with the vegetables and enough stock to barely cover the meat and vegetables. Bring to a boil, then reduce the heat, cover the pot, and cook in the oven for 1¾–2¼ hours until the meat is very tender. Serve hot.

FREEZE AHEAD

To make ahead and freeze, complete the recipe to the end of step 4, without the garnish. Cool quickly and put into a freezer container. Seal and freeze for up to one month. To use, thaw overnight at cool room temperature. Heat the oven to 350°F (325°F convection oven). Put the stew into a Dutch oven, add an extra ⅔ cup (160ml) beef stock and bring to a boil. Cover and reheat for 30 minutes.

Serves 6

Perfect Roasting

Succulent roasts are simple once you know how. When the roast is cooked to your liking, make sure it has time to rest before carving to let the juices redistribute themselves throughout the meat for moist, tender results.

Roasting know-how

- ❑ Let the meat come to room temperature before cooking—remove from the refrigerator 1–2 hours ahead.
- ❑ Cook on a wire rack, or on a bed of sliced vegetables, so the fat drips away.
- ❑ Roast fat-side up.
- ❑ During roasting, check the juices in the roasting pan to make sure they don't dry up and scorch—this will ruin the gravy. Pour a little freshly boiled water or stock into the roasting pan, if necessary.

- ❑ When cooked, transfer the meat to a warm plate or dish, cover loosely with aluminum foil, and leave to rest before carving. This makes the meat juicier and easier to carve. Leave the meat to rest for at least 15 minutes. A large roast can rest for 45 minutes without getting cold.

Seasoning

All roasts can be seasoned before roasting for extra flavor. Use salt and freshly ground black pepper, or a dry marinade (see below).

1 Rub the roast with vegetable oil to help the seasonings stick.
2 Press on the seasonings in a thin, uniform layer.

Dry marinades

These don't penetrate far into the meat, but give an excellent flavor on and just under the crust. Make them with crushed garlic, dried herbs or spices, and plenty of freshly ground black pepper. Rub into the meat and then leave to marinate in the refrigerator for at least 30 minutes, or up to 8 hours before roasting.

Roast Rib of Beef

Prep time: 5 minutes
Cooking time: about 2¾ hours, plus resting

2-bone standing rib of beef roast (weight 5½–6lb./2.5–2.7kg)

1 tbsp. all-purpose flour

1 tbsp. mustard powder

⅔ cup (160ml) dry red wine

2½ cups (600ml) beef stock

2½ cups (600ml) vegetable stock

salt and freshly ground black pepper

fresh thyme sprigs to garnish

roasted root vegetables (optional) to serve

1 Heat the oven to 450°F (400°F convection oven). Put the beef, fat-side up, in a roasting pan just large enough to hold the roast. Mix the flour and mustard together in a small bowl and season with salt and ground black pepper, then rub the mixture over the beef. Roast in the middle of the oven for 30 minutes.

2 Move the beef to a lower shelf, near the bottom of the oven. Reduce the oven temperature to 425°F (400°F convection oven) and continue to roast the beef for 2 hours longer, basting occasionally.

3 Transfer the beef to a carving dish, cover loosely with aluminum foil, and leave to rest while you make the gravy. Skim off most of the fat from the roasting pan. Put the roasting pan on the stovetop over high heat, pour in the wine, and boil vigorously until very syrupy. Pour in the stock, bring to a boil again, and boil until syrupy. Add the vegetable stock and continue boiling until syrupy. There should be about 2 cups (500ml) gravy. Taste and adjust the seasoning.

4 Remove the rib bones and carve the beef. Garnish with thyme and serve with roasted vegetables, if you like.

SAVE TIME

Buy the best-quality meat you can afford. The beef should be a dark red color, not bright red, and have a good marbling of fat throughout.

Serves 8

Perfect Cold Roast Beef

Prep time: 15 minutes, plus overnight chilling
Cooking time: about 2 hours

4½lb. (2kg) rolled boneless top round roast

2 tbsp. light brown soft sugar

1 tbsp. mustard powder

1 tbsp. vegetable oil

coleslaw, watercress leaves, and creamed horseradish to serve

1 Take the beef out of the refrigerator 1 hour before cooking to let it come to room temperature.

2 Heat the oven to 400°F (350°F convection oven). Pat the beef dry with paper towels and take a note of its weight (just in case). Mix the sugar and mustard powder together in a small bowl, then rub all over the beef. Heat the oil in a large skillet over high heat and fry the beef until brown on all sides.

3 Sit the beef in a roasting pan just large enough to hold the roast and cover loosely with foil. Roast in the oven for 15 minutes per 1lb. 2oz. (500g) for rare meat, 20 minutes per 1lb. 2oz. (500g) for medium-rare meat, or 25 minutes per 1lb. 2oz. (500g) for well-done meat, then roast for an extra 10 minutes on top of the calculated time. Or use a meat thermometer—for medium-rare meat the internal temperature of the beef should be 140°F.

4 Transfer the beef to a board and leave to cool completely. Wrap well in aluminum foil and chill overnight. (Or, to serve this beef hot as part of a buffet—just leave it to rest for 30 minutes after roasting, then carve.)

5 An hour before serving, slice the beef thinly and arrange on a serving plate, then cover. Serve with coleslaw, watercress leaves, and creamed horseradish.

SAVE TIME

Cook the beef to the end of step 3 up to three days ahead, then complete the recipe and chill.

Serves 8

Braising and Pot-Roasting

Tougher cuts require gentle, slow cooking, and braising and pot-roasting are the perfect techniques. They are similiar, but braises require more liquid.

Tips for perfect results

❑ Good cuts of beef include shank, chuck, brisket, and flank; good cuts of lamb include leg, shoulder, neck, breast, and shank.

❑ Cuts you would normally roast can also be casseroled. These simply need less time in the oven.

❑ Always use low heat and check regularly to make sure there is enough liquid to prevent the meat from sticking to the bottom of the pot.

❑ Braised dishes often improve by being cooked in advance and then slowly reheated just before serving. If you've braised a whole piece of meat, you can slice it before reheating.

Braised Lamb Shanks

To serve six, you will need:
3 tbsp. olive oil; 6 lamb shanks;
1 large onion, 3 carrots, 3 celery
stalks, each thickly sliced; 2 crushed
garlic cloves, 2 cans (15oz./425g)
crushed tomatoes; ⅔ cup (160ml)
white wine, 2 bay leaves; salt and
freshly ground black pepper

1   Heat the oven to 325°F (300°F
    convection oven). Heat the oil in
    a large Dutch oven and lightly
    brown the lamb shanks all over,
    two or three at a time. Remove
    from the pan and put to one side.
    Add the onion, carrots, celery, and
    garlic, and cook until beginning to
    color, then add the lamb, tomatoes,
    and wine.
2   Stir well, season, and add the bay
    leaves. Bring to a boil, then cover
    and transfer to the oven for
    2 hours, or until the meat is tender.
    Skim off any fat, if necessary.

Braised Lamb Shanks with Cannellini Beans

Prep time: 15 minutes
Cooking time: about 2¾ hours

3 tbsp. olive oil

6 lamb shanks

1 large onion, chopped

3 carrots, sliced

3 celery stalks, trimmed and sliced

2 garlic cloves, crushed

2 × 15oz (425g) cans crushed tomatoes

½ cup (125ml) balsamic vinegar

2 bay leaves

2 × 15oz. (425g) cans cannellini or navy beans, drained and rinsed

salt and freshly ground black pepper

1 Heat the oven to 325°F (300°F convection oven). Heat the oil in a large Dutch oven and brown the lamb shanks, in batches, all over. Remove them from the pot and put to one side.

2 Add the onion, carrots, celery, and garlic to the pot, and cook slowly until they are soft and just beginning to color.

3 Put the lamb back into the pot, add the tomatoes, vinegar, and bay leaves, and give the mixture a good stir. Season with salt and ground black pepper. Bring to a simmer, cover, and cook on the stovetop for 5 minutes.

4 Transfer to the oven and cook for 1½–2 hours until the lamb shanks are nearly tender.

5 Take the pot out of the oven and add the cannellini beans. Cover and put back into the oven for 30 minutes longer, then serve.

Serves 6

Lamb Shanks with Fruit

Prep time: about 25 minutes
Cooking time: 2¾ hours

6 small lamb shanks

1lb. (450g) whole shallots

2 eggplants, cut into small cubes

2 tbsp. olive oil

3 tbsp. harissa paste

pared zest of 1 orange and juice
  of 3 large oranges

¾ cup plus 2 tbsp. (200ml) medium
  sherry

3 cups tomato puree

1¼ cups (300ml) hot lamb stock

½ cup ready-to-eat dried apricots

½ cup pitted cherries (optional)

a large pinch of saffron threads

couscous and French beans (optional)
  to serve

1 Heat the oven to 325°F (300°F convection oven). Heat a large Dutch oven over medium heat and brown the lamb shanks all over. Allow 10–12 minutes to do this—the better the color now, the better the flavor will be in the finished dish.

2 Remove the lamb and put to one side. Add the shallots, eggplants, and oil to the pot, and cook over high heat, stirring from time to time, until the shallots and eggplant are colored and beginning to soften.

3 Reduce the heat and add the lamb and all the other ingredients, except the couscous and beans. The liquid should come halfway up the shanks. Bring to a boil, then cover tightly and put into the oven for 2½ hours. Test the lamb with a fork—it should be so tender that it almost falls off the bone.

4 If the cooking liquid looks too thin, transfer the lamb to a heated serving plate, then bubble the sauce on the stovetop until it reduces and thickens Put the lamb back into the pot and stir to combine. Serve with couscous, and French beans, if you like.

Serves 6

Italian Braised Leg of Lamb

Prep time: 15 minutes
Cooking time: about 5 hours

5lb. (2.3kg) whole boned leg of lamb, trimmed of fat

4 tbsp. olive oil

4¾ cups roughy chopped onions

1 each red, orange, and yellow bell peppers, seeded and roughly chopped

2 red chilies, seeded and finely chopped (see Safety Tip)

1 garlic bulb, cloves separated and peeled

3 tbsp. dried oregano

1 bottle (750ml) dry white wine

3 × 15oz. (425g) cans cherry tomatoes

salt and freshly ground black pepper

1 Heat the oven to 325°F (300°F convection oven). Season the lamb with salt and ground black pepper. Heat 2 tbsp. of the oil in a large Dutch oven and brown the meat well. Remove from the pot and put to one side. Wipe the pot clean.

2 Heat the remaining oil in the pot and fry the onions, chopped peppers, chilies, garlic, and oregano over medium heat for 10–15 minutes until the onions are translucent and golden brown. Stir in the wine and tomatoes and bring to a boil, then leave to bubble for 10 minutes.

3 Put the lamb on top of the vegetables and season. Baste the meat with the sauce, then cover the pot with aluminum foil and the lid. Cook in the oven for 4 hours, basting occasionally.

4 Uncover and cook for 30 minutes longer. Serve the lamb carved into thick slices with the sauce from the pot spooned over.

SAFETY TIP

Chilies vary enormously in strength, from very mild to blisteringly hot, depending on the type of chili and its ripeness. Taste a small piece first to make sure it's not too hot for you.

Be extremely careful when handling chilies not to touch or rub your eyes with your fingers, because they will sting. Wash knives immediately after cutting chilies for the same reason. As a precaution, use rubber gloves when cutting chilies, if you like.

Serves 6

Braised Beef with Pancetta and Mushrooms

Prep time: 20 minutes
Cooking time: about 3½ hours

6oz. (175g) smoked pancetta or smoked thick-cut bacon, chopped

2 leeks, trimmed and thickly sliced

1 tbsp. olive oil

1lb. (450g) braising steak, cut into 2in. (5cm) pieces

1 large onion, finely chopped

2 carrots, thickly sliced

2 parsnips, thickly sliced

1 tbsp. all-purpose flour

1¼ cups (300ml) dry red wine

1–2 tbsp. red currant jelly

1½ cups halved cremini mushrooms

freshly ground black pepper

freshly chopped flat-leaf parsley to garnish

1 Heat the oven to 325°F (300°F convection oven). Fry the pancetta or bacon in a shallow Dutch oven for 2–3 minutes until colored. Add the leeks and cook for 2 minutes longer, stirring, or until they are starting to color. Remove from the pot with a slotted spoon and put to one side. Wipe out the pot.

2 Heat the oil in the pot. Fry the beef in batches for 2–3 minutes until brown on all sides. Remove and put to one side. Add the onion and fry over low heat for 5 minutes, or until golden. Stir in the carrots and parsnips and fry for 1–2 minutes.

3 Put the beef back into the pot and stir in the flour to soak up the juices. Gradually add the wine and 1¼ cups (300ml) water, then stir in the red currant jelly. Season with ground black pepper and bring to a boil. Cover tightly, transfer to the oven, and cook for 2 hours.

4 Stir in the leeks, pancetta, and mushrooms, then re-cover and cook for 1 hour longer, or until the beef is tender. Serve hot, sprinkled with chopped parsley.

Serves 4

Braised Beef with Chestnuts and Celery

Prep time: 25 minutes
Cooking time: about 2¼ hours

18 fresh chestnuts, skins split

1 tbsp. butter

1 tbsp. vegetable oil

2 bacon slices, chopped

2lb. (900g) stewing steak, cubed

1 onion, chopped

1 tbsp. all-purpose flour

1¼ cups (300ml) brown ale

1¼ cups (300ml) beef stock

a pinch of freshly grated nutmeg

finely grated zest and juice of 1 orange

3 celery stalks, chopped

salt and freshly ground black pepper

freshly chopped flat-leaf parsley
   to garnish

1 Heat the oven to 325°F (300°F convection oven). Cook the chestnuts in a pan of simmering water for about 7 minutes. Remove from the water one at a time and peel off the outer skin and thin inner skin while still warm.

2 Melt the butter with the oil in a Dutch oven. Add the bacon and beef in batches and cook, stirring occasionally, until brown. Remove the meat with a slotted spoon.

3 Add the onion to the pot and fry, stirring, until soft. Drain off most of the fat. Put the meat back into the pot, sprinkle in the flour, and cook, stirring, for 1–2 minutes.

4 Stir in the brown ale, stock, nutmeg, and the orange juice and half the zest, and season to taste. Bring to a boil, then stir well to loosen the sediment and add the chestnuts. Cover tightly with aluminum foil and the lid and cook in the oven for about 45 minutes.

5 After 45 minutes, add the celery to the pot, re-cover, and cook for 1 hour longer, or until the meat is tender. Serve with the remaining orange zest and the parsley sprinkled over the top.

Serves 6

Smoky Goulash

Prep time: 20 minutes
Cooking time: about 3 hours

2½lb. (1.2kg) braising steak

3 tbsp. olive oil, plus extra to drizzle

16 whole shallots or button onions

1½ cups roughly chopped chorizo
    sausage

1 red chili, seeded and chopped
    (see Safety Tip, page 119)

3 bay leaves

3 garlic cloves, crushed

2 tbsp. all-purpose flour

2 tbsp. smoked paprika

3 cups plus 2 tbsp. (700ml) tomato puree

7 tbsp. hot beef stock

salt and freshly ground black pepper

mashed potatoes and green vegetables
    to serve

For the minted sour cream

1¼ cups (300ml) sour cream

1 tbsp. finely chopped fresh mint

1 tbsp. extra virgin olive oil, plus extra
    to drizzle

1 Mix together all the ingredients for the minted sour cream and season with a little salt and plenty of coarsely ground black pepper. Cover and chill in the refrigerator until needed.

2 Heat the oven to 325°F (300°F convection oven). Cut the braising steak into large cubes, slightly larger than bite-size pieces.

3 Heat the oil in a large Dutch oven until really hot. Brown the beef, a few cubes at a time, over high heat until they are deep brown all over. Remove each batch with a slotted spoon and put to one side. Repeat with the remaining beef cubes until all the pieces are brown.

4 Reduce the heat, then add the shallots or button onions, the chorizo, chili, bay leaves, and garlic. Fry for 7–10 minutes until the shallots are golden brown and beginning to become soft. Put the meat back into the pot, then stir in the all-purpose flour and paprika. Cook, stirring, for 1–2

minutes, then add the tomato puree and season.

5 Cover the pot and cook in the oven for 2½ hours, or until the beef is meltingly tender. Check halfway through cooking—if the beef looks dry, add the hot stock. Serve with the minted sour cream, drizzled with a little olive oil and sprinkled with black pepper, and some creamy mashed potatoes and green vegetables alongside.

SAVE TIME

Complete the recipe, cool, and chill up to three days ahead, or freeze for up to one month. To use, if frozen, thaw overnight at a cool room temperature. Put the goulash back into the Dutch oven, bring to a boil, reduce the heat, and simmer for 15–20 minutes until piping hot, adding 7 tbsp. hot beef stock if the mixture looks too dry.

Serves 8

Steak and Onion Puff Pie

Prep time: 30 minutes
Cooking time: about 2½ hours

3 tbsp. vegetable oil

2 onions, sliced

2lb. (900g) beef, chopped

3 tbsp. all-purpose flour, plus extra
to dust

2 cups (500ml) beef stock

2 fresh rosemary sprigs, bruised

1lb. 2oz. (500g) puff pastry dough

1 egg, beaten, to glaze

salt and freshly ground black pepper

1 Heat the oven to 325°F (300°F convection oven).

2 Heat 1 tbsp. of the oil in a large Dutch oven or other flameproof pan with a lid. Fry the onions for 10 minutes, or until golden brown. Lift out and put to one side. Sear the meat in the same pot, in batches, using more oil as necessary, until brown all over. Lift out each batch as soon as it is brown and put to one side. Add the flour to the pot and stir for 1–2 minutes to brown. Put the onions and beef back into the pot, add the beef stock and the rosemary, and season well with salt and ground black pepper. Cover and bring to a boil, then cook in the oven for 1½ hours, or until the meat is tender.

3 About 30 minutes before the end of the cooking time, lightly dust a work surface with flour and roll out the dough. Using a 4½-cup (1.1-liter) baking dish as a template, cut out dough lid. Put on a cookie sheet and chill until needed.

4 Take the pot out of the oven. Increase the oven temperature to 425°F (400°F convection oven). Pour the beef mixture into the baking dish, brush the edges with water, and cover with the dough lid. Press lightly to seal. Lightly score the top and brush with the egg. Put the dish back on the cookie sheet and bake for 30 minutes, or until the pastry is risen and golden. Serve the pie immediately.

FREEZE AHEAD

To make ahead and freeze, complete the recipe to the end of step 3. Cool the casserole quickly. Put the beef mixture into a freezer dish. Brush the dish edge with water, cover with the dough, and press to seal. Score the dough. Cover with plastic wrap and freeze for up to three months.

To use, thaw overnight at cool room temperature or in the refrigerator. Brush the dough with beaten egg, then bake in an oven heated to 425°F (400°F convection oven) for 35 minutes, or until the pastry is brown and the filling piping hot.

Serves 4

Slow-Cooker Suppers

Perfect Slow Cooker

A slow cooker is ideal for the cook with a busy lifestyle. We might relish the stews and casseroles our grandmothers would have prepared for midweek meals without a second thought, but now they're more of a treat for weekends when we have more time to spend in the kitchen. A slow cooker, however, solves that problem: switch it on as you leave in the morning and you'll return home to a delicious, homecooked meal.

What is a slow cooker and how does it work?

A slow cooker is a standalone electrical appliance designed to be plugged in and left gently cooking unsupervised for hours, without the food burning or drying up. It consists of a lidded round or oval earthenware or ceramic pot that sits in a metal housing containing the heating element, which heats the contents to a steady temperature of about 212°F. Little steam can escape and it condenses in the lid, forming a seal that keeps the temperature constant and the food moist.

Depending on the model, there will be two or three cooking settings (Low, Medium, and High) and a "Keep Warm" function. These settings give you the option to cook a dish on High for just a few hours or on Low all day or overnight. Multifunctional models can also be used as rice cookers and steamers. Older-style slow cookers have a fixed pot to contain the food, but, nowadays, most contain a removable, dishwasher-friendly pot that can be taken straight to the table for serving.

Want to save on dish washing? Choose a removable pot that can be used to start off the dish on the stovetop and then transferred to the slow cooker unit. Alternatively, use slow cooker liners (available from speciality cooking websites) if you have a fixed-pot slow cooker.

Choosing a slow cooker

Anyone can use a slow cooker: some models are ideal for large families or the cook who likes to stock the freezer, while smaller versions are suitable for couples or for students living in studio apartments. Otherwise, choose yours according to what you most like to cook: are you only planning to use it for casseroles, will you want to cook a whole chicken, or are you hoping to make plenty of desserts? Be sure to think about the size and shape before you buy.

What you can cook in a slow cooker?

Practically anything! Don't just stick to soups, stews, and casseroles. You can keep gravy warm (a great Thanksgiving stovetop space-saver, for example), braise joints of meat and whole chickens, and even bake cakes and make pâtés. Set it to cook overnight and you can enjoy a bowl of warm oatmeal for breakfast, too. Cooking food in a slow cooker has many benefits: flavors have time to develop and even the toughest of cuts of meat become incredibly tender. It's important, however, to raise the temperature quickly to destroy harmful bacteria in raw meat, poultry, and fish, so either bring the food to boiling point on the stovetop first or preheat the slow cooker—always follow the manufacturer's directions.

What you can't cook in a slow cooker?

Not much! But obviously very large meat pieces and whole poultry, such as turkey aren't suitable, and roasts and stir-fries are out of the question. Some foods, such as pasta, rice, fish, puddings, and cakes, are only suitable for shorter slow cooking times, so always check the recipe. Milk and cream will separate if cooked for a long time—add them to finish off and enrich a dish in the last few minutes of the cooking time. Always fully immerse potatoes to stop them blackening while cooking.

Saving money with a slow cooker

Not only are slow cookers practical, they're also economical.

❑ Tougher cuts of meat, such as oxtail, beef or lamb shanks, tend to be the less-expensive cuts and benefit from long, slow cooking at low temperatures. They are all perfect for the slow cooker.

❑ Slow cookers use far less energy than a conventional oven, because you are only heating up a small piece of equipment that runs on a minute amount of power in comparison.

❑ They're ideal for flexible meal times, saving you cash and conserving energy. A slow cooker is especially useful for large, active families where everyone eats at different times—prepare one dish, then keep it warm in the pot for up to two hours.

Slow cooker safety tips

❑ Always stand the appliance on a heat-resistant surface.

❑ Do not use a slow cooker to reheat cold or frozen food—the temperature rises too slowly to kill harmful bacteria. Heat the food first on the stovetop, then transfer it to the slow cooker pot.

❑ Always use oven mitts to remove the pot from the slow cooker.

❑ Never immerse the outer housing in water; stand it on a draining board to clean, and remove the cord if possible.

❑ Never fill the outer housing with food; always use the inner pot.

❑ Don't let young children touch the slow cooker—the housing and the lid can become very hot or spit boiling water.

❑ Be careful when cooking with dried beans—kidney beans, for example, need to be boiled vigorously for 10 minutes to remove harmful toxins. Do this in a pan on the stovetop before draining and continuing with the recipe in the slow cooker.

Mexican Bean Soup

Prep time: 15 minutes

Cooking time: 10 minutes in pan, then about 3 hours on High, plus cooling

---

4 tbsp. olive oil

1 onion, chopped

2 garlic cloves, chopped

a pinch of crushed dried red chilies

1 tsp. ground coriander

1 tsp. ground cumin

½ tsp. ground cinnamon

2½ cups (600ml) hot vegetable stock

1¼ cups (300ml) tomato juice

1–2 tsp. chili sauce

2 × 15oz. (425g) cans red kidney beans, drained and rinsed

2 tbsp. freshly chopped cilantro

salt and freshly ground black pepper

fresh cilantro leaves, roughly torn, to garnish

crusty bread and lime butter to serve (optional, see below)

Lime Butter

Beat the grated zest and juice of ½ lime into 4 tbsp. soft butter and season to taste. Shape into a log, wrap in plastic wrap, and chill until needed. To serve, unwrap and slice thinly.

1 Heat the oil in a large pan, add the onion, garlic, chilies, and spices, and fry slowly for 5 minutes, or until light golden.

2 Add the hot stock, the tomato juice, chili sauce, and beans, and bring to a boil. Transfer to the slow cooker, cover, and cook on High for 2–3 hours.

3 Leave the soup to cool a little, then blend in batches in a blender or food processor until very smooth. Pour the soup into a clean pan, stir in the chopped cilantro, and heat through slowly on the stovetop—do not boil. Season to taste with salt and ground black pepper.

4 Ladle the soup into warm bowls. Top each portion with a few slices of lime butter, if you like, and scatter with torn cilantro leaves.

Scotch Broth

Prep time: 15 minutes
Cooking time: 20 minutes in pan, then about 10 hours on Low

3lb. (1.4kg) piece beef skirt steak

1½ cups dried bean soup mix—include pearl barley, red lentils, split peas, and green peas—soaked according to the package directions and drained

2 carrots, finely chopped

1 parsnip, finely chopped

2 onions, finely chopped

¼ white cabbage, finely chopped

1 leek, trimmed and finely chopped

1 piece marrow bone (weight about 12oz./350g)

½ tbsp. salt

freshly ground black pepper

2 tbsp. freshly chopped parsley and crusty bread to serve

1 Put the beef into a large pan and cover with water. Slowly bring to a boil, then reduce the heat and simmer for 10 minutes, using a slotted spoon to remove any scum that comes to the surface. Drain.

2 Put the soup mix and the vegetables into the slow cooker, then place the beef and marrow bone on top. Add 6 cups (1.4 liters) boiling water—there should be enough to just cover the meat. Cover and cook on Low for 8–10 hours until the meat is tender.

3 Remove the marrow bone and beef from the broth. Add a few shreds of beef to the broth, if you like. Season the broth well with the salt and some ground black pepper, then stir in the chopped parsley and serve hot with crusty bread.

SAVE EFFORT

This can be two meals in one: a first course and a main course. The beef flavors the stock and is removed before serving. You can then divide up the meat and serve it with mashed potatoes.

Serves 8

Easy Chicken Casserole

Prep time: 15 minutes
Cooking time: 10 minutes in pan, then about 6 hours on Low

1 tbsp. sunflower oil

3lb. (4kg) chicken

1 fresh rosemary sprig

2 bay leaves

1 red onion, cut into wedges

2 carrots, cut into chunks

2 leeks, trimmed and cut into chunks

2 celery stalks, cut into chunks

12 baby new potatoes, halved if large

3¾ cups (900ml) hot chicken stock

7oz. (200g) green beans, trimmed

salt and freshly ground black pepper

1 Heat the oil in a large pan over medium heat. Add the chicken and fry until brown all over. Put the chicken into the slow cooker, along with the herbs and all the vegetables, except the green beans. Season well.

2 Pour in the hot stock, cover, and cook on Low for 5–6 hours until the chicken is cooked through. Add the beans for the last hour, or cook separately in lightly salted boiling water and stir into the casserole once it's cooked. To test the chicken is cooked, pierce the thickest part of the leg with a knife; the juices should run clear.

3 Remove the chicken and spoon the vegetables into six bowls. Carve the chicken and divide among the bowls, then ladle the cooking liquid over.

SAVE EFFORT

For a different serving suggestion, omit the baby new potatoes and serve with mashed potatoes.

Serves 6

Spanish Chicken

Prep time: 25 minutes, plus infusing
Cooking time: about 20 minutes in pan, then about 2 hours on Low

1 tsp. ground turmeric

4½ cups (1.1 liters) hot chicken stock

2 tbsp. vegetable oil

4 boneless, skinless chicken thighs, roughly diced

1 onion, chopped

1 red bell pepper, seeded and sliced

½ cup diced chorizo sausage

2 garlic cloves, crushed

1½ cups long-grain rice

scant 1 cup frozen peas

salt and freshly ground black pepper

3 tbsp. freshly chopped flat-leaf parsley to garnish

crusty bread to serve

1. Add the turmeric to the hot stock and leave to infuse for at least 5 minutes. Meanwhile, heat the oil in a large skillet over medium heat. Add the chicken and fry for 10 minutes, or until golden, then transfer to the slow cooker.

2. Add the onion to the pan and cook over medium heat for 5 minutes, or until soft. Add the red pepper and chorizo and cook for 5 minutes longer, then add the garlic and cook for 1 minute, stirring.

3. Add the rice and mix well. Pour in the stock, add the peas, and season, then transfer to the slow cooker and stir together. Cover and cook on Low for 1–2 hours until the rice is tender and the chicken is cooked through.

4. Check the seasoning and garnish with the parsley. Serve with some crusty bread.

Serves 4

Chicken Tagine with Apricots and Almonds

Slow Cooker Recipe

Prep time: 10 minutes
Cooking time: about 15 minutes in pan, then about 5 hours on Low

2 tbsp. olive oil

4 chicken thighs

1 onion, chopped

2 tsp. ground cinnamon

2 tbsp. honey

1 cup ready-to-eat dried apricots

⅔ cup blanched almonds

½ cup (125ml) hot chicken stock

salt and freshly ground black pepper

slivered almonds to garnish

couscous to serve

1. Heat 1 tbsp. of the oil in a large pan over medium heat. Add the chicken and fry for 5 minutes, or until brown, then transfer to the slow cooker.

2. Add the onion to the pan with the remaining oil and fry for 10 minutes, or until soft.

3. Add the cinnamon, honey, apricots, almonds, and hot stock to the onion, and season well. Bring to a boil, then transfer to the slow cooker, cover, and cook on Low for 4–5 hours until the chicken is tender and cooked through. Garnish with the slivered almonds and serve hot with couscous.

Serves 4

Chicken with Chorizo and Beans

🍴 **Prep time:** 10 minutes
Cooking time: about 20 minutes in pan, then about 5 hours on Low

1 tbsp. olive oil

12 chicken pieces (6 drumsticks and 6 thighs)

1 cup cubed chorizo sausage

1 onion, finely chopped

2 large garlic cloves, crushed

1 tsp. mild chili powder

3 red bell peppers, seeded and roughly chopped

1¾ cups (400ml) tomato puree

2 tbsp. tomato paste

⅔ cup (160ml) hot chicken stock

2 cans (15-oz./425g) butter beans or fava beans, drained and rinsed

7oz. (200g) new potatoes, quartered

1 small bunch of fresh thyme

1 bay leaf

7oz. (200g) baby leaf spinach

SAVE EFFORT

An easy way to get a brand new dish is to use mixed beans instead of butter beans.

1 Heat the oil in a large skillet over medium heat. Add the chicken pieces and fry in batches until brown all over, then put to one side.

2 Add the chorizo to the skillet and fry for 2–3 minutes until its oil starts to run. Add the onion, garlic, and chili powder, and fry over low heat for 5 minutes, or until the onion is soft.

3 Add the red peppers and cook for 2–3 minutes longer until soft. Stir in the tomato puree, tomato paste, hot stock, butter beans, potatoes, thyme sprigs, and bay leaf. Bring to a boil, then add to the chicken. Cover and cook on Low for 4–5 hours until the chicken is cooked through.

4 Remove the thyme and bay leaf, then stir in the spinach until it wilts. Serve immediately.

Serves 6

Mexican Chili Con Carne

Slow Cooker Recipe

Prep time: 5 minutes

Cooking time: 25 minutes in pan, then about 5 hours on Low

2 tbsp. olive oil

1lb. (450g) ground beef

1 large onion, finely chopped

½–1 tsp. cayene pepper

½–1 tsp. ground cumin

3 tbsp. tomato paste

⅔ cup (160ml) hot beef stock

15oz. (425g) can crushed tomatoes with garlic (see Save Time)

1oz. (25g) dark chocolate

15oz. (425g) can red kidney beans, drained and rinsed

1½oz. (40g) fresh cilantro, chopped

salt and freshly ground black pepper

guacamole, salsa, sour cream, grated cheese, tortilla chips, and pickled chilies to serve

SAVE TIME

If you can't find a can of tomatoes with garlic, use a can of crushed tomatoes and 1 crushed garlic clove.

1 Heat 1 tbsp. of the oil in a large skillet and fry the beef for 10 minutes, or until brown, stirring to break up any lumps. Remove the beef from the pan with a slotted spoon and transfer to the slow cooker.

2 Add the remaining oil to the pan, then fry the onion, stirring, for 10 minutes, or until soft and golden.

3 Add the spices and fry for 1 minute longer, then add the tomato paste, hot stock, and the tomatoes. Bring to a boil, then stir into the beef in the slow cooker. Cover and cook on Low for 4–5 hours.

4 Stir in the chocolate, kidney beans, and cilantro, and season with salt and ground black pepper. Leave to stand for 10 minutes.

5 Serve with guacamole, salsa, sour cream, grated cheese, tortilla chips, and pickled chilies.

Serves 4

Beef Goulash

Slow Cooker Recipe

Prep time: 30 minutes

Cooking time: about 20 minutes in pan, then about 10 hours on Low

---

2 tbsp. all-purpose flour

2¼lb. (1kg) stewing steak, cut into 1¼in. (3cm) cubes

3 tbsp. vegetable oil

4⅔ cups chopped onions

1½ cups diced pancetta

2 garlic cloves, crushed

4 tbsp. paprika

2 tsp. Italian herbs

15oz. (425g) can peeled plum tomatoes

⅔ cup (160ml) hot beef stock

⅔ cup (160ml) sour cream

salt and freshly ground black pepper

freshly chopped flat-leaf parsley to garnish

noodles to serve

---

1 Put the flour into a resealable plastic bag and season with salt and ground black pepper, then toss the beef in the flour to coat and shake off any excess.

2 Heat 2 tbsp. of the oil in a large skillet and quickly fry the meat in small batches until brown on all sides. Transfer to the slow cooker.

3 Heat the remaining oil in the pan, add the onions, and fry for 5–7 minutes until they are becoming soft and and turning golden. Add the pancetta and fry over high heat until crisp. Stir in the garlic and paprika and cook, stirring, for 1 minute.

4 Add the herbs, tomatoes, and hot stock, and bring to a boil. Stir into the beef in the slow cooker, then cover and cook on Low for 8–10 hours until the beef is tender.

5 Check the seasoning, then stir in the sour cream. Garnish with parsley and serve with noodles.

Serves 6

Beef and Stout Stew

Slow Cooker Recipe

Prep time: 15 minutes
Cooking time: 25 minutes in pan, then about 10 hours on Low

2 tbsp. all-purpose flour

3lb. (1.4kg) boneless beef shank
or braising steak, cut into 1¼in. (3cm)
cubes

4 tbsp. vegetable oil

2 onions, sliced

4 carrots, cut into chunks

1 cup (240ml) dark ale

1¼ cups (300ml) hot beef stock

2 bay leaves

1½lb. (700g) new potatoes, halved
if large

2 tbsp. freshly chopped flat-leaf parsley

salt and freshly ground black pepper

mashed potatoes, snow peas, and peas
to serve

1 Put the flour into a resealable plastic
bag, season with salt and ground
black pepper, and toss the beef in
the flour to coat, then shake off any
excess. Heat the oil in a large skillet
until hot. Add a handful of beef and
fry until brown all over. Remove with
a slotted spoon and transfer to the
slow cooker, then repeat until all the
meat is brown.

2 Add the onions and carrots to the
pan and cook for 10 minutes, or
until brown. Add the ale, scraping
the bottom of the pan to loosen
the browned bits, then stir in the
hot stock. Add the bay leaves and
potatoes and bring to a boil. Pour
over the beef in the slow cooker,
then cover and cook on Low for 8–10
hours until the beef is tender.

3 Stir in the chopped parsley and
season to taste with salt and ground
black pepper, and serve with mashed
potatoes, snow peas, and peas.

Pheasant Casserole with Cider and Apples

Prep time: 50 minutes

Cooking time: about 25 minutes in pan, then about 7 hours on Low

2 large, oven-ready pheasants

2 tbsp. all-purpose flour, plus extra to dust

4 tbsp. butter

4 bacon slices, halved

2 onions, chopped

2 celery stalks, chopped

1 tbsp. dried juniper berries, lightly crushed

1in. (2.5cm) piece ginger root, peeled and finely chopped

⅔ cup (160ml) hot pheasant or chicken stock (see page 44)

1½ cups (350ml) hard cider or apple juice

⅔ cup (160ml) heavy cream

4 crisp dessert apples

1 tbsp. lemon juice

salt and freshly ground black pepper

1 Cut each pheasant into four portions, then season with salt and ground black pepper and dust with flour.

2 Melt three-quarters of the butter in a large skillet and brown the pheasant portions, in batches, over high heat until deep golden brown all over. Transfer to the slow cooker.

3 Add the bacon to the pan and fry for 2–3 minutes until golden. Add the onions, celery, juniper berries, and ginger and cook for 8–10 minutes.

4 Stir in the remaining flour and cook, stirring, for 2 minutes, then add the hot stock and the cider and bring to a boil, stirring. Pour into the slow cooker and season well, then cover and cook on Low for 6–7 hours until the pheasant is tender.

5 Lift out the pheasant and put into a warmed dish and keep it warm. Strain the sauce through a sieve into a pan. Stir in the cream, bring to the boil and bubble for 10 minutes or until syrupy.

6 Quarter, core and cut the apples into wedges, then toss in the lemon juice. Melt the remaining butter in a small pan and fry the apple wedges for 2–3 minutes until golden. Put the pheasant back into the sauce, along with the apples, and check the seasoning before serving.

Serves 8

Curried Lamb with Lentils

Slow Cooker Recipe

Prep time: 15 minutes, plus marinating
Cooking time: 20 minutes in pan, then about 6 hours on Low

1lb. 2oz. (500g) lean stewing lamb on the bone, cut into 8 pieces (ask a butcher to do this), trimmed of fat

1 tsp. ground cumin

1 tsp. ground turmeric

2 garlic cloves, crushed

1 medium red chili, seeded and chopped (see Safety Tip, page 119)

1in. (2.5cm) piece of ginger root, peeled and grated

2 tbsp. vegetable oil

1 onion, chopped

15oz. (425g) can crushed tomatoes

2 tbsp. vinegar

scant 1 cup red lentils, rinsed

salt and freshly ground black pepper

cilantro sprigs to garnish

arugula salad to serve

1 Put the lamb into a shallow container and add the spices, garlic, chili, ginger, salt and ground black pepper. Stir well to mix, then cover and chill for at least 30 minutes.

2 Heat the oil in a large skillet, add the onion, and cook over low heat for 5 minutes until soft. Add the lamb and cook for 10 minutes, turning regularly, or until the meat is evenly brown.

3 Add the tomatoes, vinegar, lentils, and 1 cup (240ml) boiling water and bring to a boil. Season well. Transfer to the slow cooker, cover, and cook on Low for 5–6 hours until the lamb is tender.

4 Serve hot, garnished with cilantro, with an arugula salad.

Serves 4

Delicious Desserts

Chocolate and Hazelnut Meringues

Prep time: 25 minutes, plus softening
Cooking time: 2 hours 10 minutes, plus cooling

⅔ cup shelled hazelnuts

heaped ½ cup superfine sugar

3oz. (75g) dark chocolate (at least 70% cocoa solids)

2 egg whites

1¼ cups (300ml) heavy cream

red currants, blackberries, and chocolate shavings to decorate

1 Heat the oven to 225°F (195°F convection oven) and heat the broiler. Line two cookie sheets with parchment paper. Spread the hazelnuts over a cookie sheet and toast under the hot grill until golden brown, turning them frequently. Put the hazelnuts into a dish towel and rub off the skins, then put the nuts into a food processor with 3 tbsp. of the sugar and process to a fine powder. Add the chocolate and pulse until roughly chopped.

2 Put the egg whites into a clean, grease-free bowl and beat until stiff. Beat in the remaining sugar, a little at a time, until it is stiff and shiny. Fold in the nut mixture.

3 Spoon the mixture onto the prepared cookie sheets, making small, rough mounds about 3½in. (9cm) across. Bake for about 45 minutes until the meringues will just peel off the paper. Gently push in the bottom of each meringue to form a deep hollow, then put back into the oven for 1¼ hours, or until crisp and dry. Leave to cool.

4 Whip the cream until it just holds its shape, then spoon three-quarters onto the meringues. Leave in the refrigerator to soften for up to 2 hours.

5 Decorate the meringues with the remaining cream, the fruit, and chocolate shavings. Serve immediately.

SAVE TIME

Complete the recipe to the end
of step 3, then store the meringues
in an airtight container up to one
week ahead. Complete steps 4 and
5 to finish the recipe.

Serves 6

Orange and Chocolate Cheesecake

Prep time: 45 minutes
Cooking time: about 2¼ hours, plus cooling

2 sticks chilled unsalted butter,
    plus extra to grease

1⅔ cups all-purpose flour, sifted

¾ cup packed light brown sugar

3 tbsp. unsweetened cocoa powder

chocolate curls to decorate
    (see opposite)

For the topping

2 oranges

1¾lb. (800g) cream cheese

1 cup plus 2 tbsp. mascarpone

4 extra-large eggs

heaped 1 cup superfine sugar

2 tbsp. cornstarch

½ tsp. vanilla extract

1 vanilla bean

1 Heat the oven to 350°F (325°F convection oven). Grease a 9in. (23cm) springform cake pan and line the bottom with parchment paper.

2 Cut 1½ sticks of the butter into cubes. Melt the remaining butter and put to one side. Put the flour and cubed butter into a food processor with the brown sugar and cocoa powder and pulse until the texture of fine bread crumbs. (Alternatively, cut the butter into the flour in a large bowl using a pastry blender. Stir in the sugar and cocoa.) Pour in the melted butter and pulse, or stir with a fork, until the mixture comes together.

3 Spoon the crumb mixture into the prepared pan and press evenly onto the bottom, using the back of a metal spoon to smooth the surface. Bake for 35–40 minutes until lightly puffed; avoid overbrowning or the cookie crust will have a bitter flavor. Take out of the oven and leave the crust to cool in the pan. Reduce the oven temperature to 300°F (250°F convection oven).

4 Meanwhile, make the topping. Grate the zest from the oranges, then squeeze the juice—you will need ⅔ cup (160ml). Put the cream cheese, mascarpone, eggs, sugar, cornstarch,

grated orange zest, and vanilla extract into a large bowl. Using a hand-held electric mixer, beat the ingredients together thoroughly until combined.

5 Split the vanilla bean in half lengthwise and, using the tip of a sharp knife, scrape out the seeds and add them to the cheese mixture. Beat in the orange juice and continue beating until the mixture is smooth.

6 Pour the cheese mixture over the cool cookie crust. Bake for about 1½ hours until pale golden on top, slightly risen, and just set around the edge. The cheesecake should still be slightly wobbly in the middle; it will set as it cools. Turn off the oven and leave the cheesecake inside, with the door ajar, to cool for 1 hour. Remove and leave to cool completely (about 3 hours), then chill in the refrigerator.

7 Just before serving, unclip the pan and transfer the cheesecake to a plate. Scatter chocolate curls on top to decorate, if you like.

Chocolate Curls

Melt some chocolate, then spread it out in a thin layer on a marble slab or clean work surface. Leave to become firm. Using a sharp blade, scrape through the chocolate at a 45-degree angle.

Serves 4

Fruity Rice Pudding

Prep time: 10 minutes
Cooking time: about 3 hours on Low, plus cooling and chilling (optional)

heaped ½ cup short-grain pudding rice

4½ cups (1.1 liters) whole milk

1 tsp. vanilla extract

3–4 tbsp. sugar

¾ cup plus 2 tbsp. (200ml) whipping cream

6 tbsp. wild lingonberry sauce, or raspberry or strawberry sauce

1 Put the rice into the slow cooker with the milk, vanilla, and sugar. Cover and cook on Low for 2–3 hours. You can enjoy the pudding hot now or leave it to cool and continue the recipe.

2 Lightly whip the cream and fold through the pudding. Chill for 1 hour.

3 Divide the rice mixture among six glass dishes and top each with 1 tbsp. lingonberry sauce.

WITHOUT A SLOW COOKER

Put the rice into a pan with 2½ cups (600ml) cold water. Bring to a boil, then reduce the heat and simmer until the liquid evaporates. Add the milk, return to a boil, then reduce the heat and simmer for 45 minutes, or until soft and creamy. Leave to cool, then complete steps 2 and 3 to finish the recipe.

SAVE EFFORT

For an alternative presentation, serve in tumblers, layering the rice pudding with the fruit sauce; you will need to use double the amount of fruit sauce.

Serves 6

Winter Fruit Compote

Prep time: 10 minutes
Cooking time: 5 minutes in pan, then about 4 hours on Low

½ cup ready-to-eat dried pears

½ cup ready-to-eat dried figs

½ cup ready-to-eat dried apricots

½ cup ready-to-eat prunes

1 star anise

½ cinnamon stick

1¼ cups (300ml) apple juice

1¼ cups (300ml) dry white wine

light brown sugar to taste (optional)

crème fraîche, sour cream, or thick
  Greek yogurt to serve

1 Put the dried fruits into the slow cooker with the star anise and cinnamon stick.

2 Pour the apple juice and wine into a pan and bring to a boil. Pour over the fruit, cover, and cook on Low for 3–4 hours until plump and tender.

3 Sprinkle the sugar over the fruit, if you like, and serve the compote with crème fraîche, sour cream, or thick Greek yogurt.

WITHOUT A SLOW COOKER

Put the dried fruits, spices, apple juice, and wine into a pan, and bring to a boil slowly. Reduce the heat, cover, and simmer for 45 minutes, or until the fruits are plump and tender. Top up the liquid, if necessary. Continue with step 3 to finish the recipe.

SAVE EFFORT

For an easy way to get a brand new dish, replace the figs with dried apple rings and the pears with raisins.

Serves 6

Plum Pudding

Prep time: 20 minutes, plus soaking
Cooking time: 8½ hours

slightly heaped 1¼ cups dried currants

slightly heaped ¼ cups golden raisins

slightly heaped 1¼ cups raisins

½ cup dried cranberries or cherries

grated zest and juice of 1 orange

4 tbsp. rum

4 tbsp. brandy

1–2 tsp. Angostura bitters

1 small apple

1 carrot

3 cups fresh bread crumbs

⅔ cup all-purpose flour, sifted

1 tsp. apple pie spice

¾ cup grated light vegetarian suet

½ cup dark brown sugar

4 tbsp. blanched almonds,
    roughly chopped

2 large eggs

butter to grease

fresh or frozen cranberries (thawed
    if frozen), fresh bay leaves, and
    confectioners' sugar to decorate

Hard Sauce to serve (see opposite)

1 Put the dried fruit and orange zest and juice into a large bowl. Pour the rum, brandy, and Angostura bitters over. Cover and leave to soak in a cool place for at least 1 hour, or overnight.

2 Peel and grate the apple and carrot, then add both to the bowl of soaked fruit with the bread crumbs, flour, apple pie spice, suet, sugar, almonds, and eggs. Mix everything together well.

3 Grease a 2-quart (2-litre) pudding bowl or heatproof bowl and line with a 24in. (60cm) square of cheesecloth. Spoon the batter into the bowl and smooth the surface. Gather the cloth up and over the top, twist, and secure with string. Put the bowl on an upturned heatproof saucer or trivet in the bottom of a large pan, then pour in enough boiling water to come halfway up the side of the bowl. Cover the pan with a tight-fitting lid and bring the water to a boil, then turn down the heat and simmer for 6 hours. Top up with more boiling water as necessary.

4 Remove the bowl from the pan and leave to cool. When the pudding is cold, remove it from the bowl, then wrap it in plastic wrap and a double layer of aluminum foil. Store in a cool, dry place for up to six months.

5 To reheat, steam for 2½ hours; check the water level every 40 minutes and top up with boiling water, if necessary. Leave the pudding in the pan, covered, to keep warm until needed.

Decorate with cranberries and bay leaves, dust with confectioners' sugar and serve with Hard Sauce.

Hard Sauce

Put 1 stick unsalted butter into a bowl and beat until very soft. Gradually beat in ½ cup sifted light brown sugar until very light and fluffy, then beat in 6 tbsp. brandy, a spoonful at a time. Cover and chill for at least 3 hours.

Serves 12

Rich Fruit Cake

Prep time: 30 minutes
Cooking time: about 2½ hours, plus cooling

1½ sticks unsalted butter, cubed, plus
  extra to grease

2¼lb. (1kg) mixed dried fruit

⅔ cup roughly chopped ready-to-eat
  dried prunes

⅓ cup roughly chopped ready-to-eat
  dried figs

⅔ cup dried cranberries

2 balls preserved stem ginger in syrup,
  grated and syrup reserved

grated zest and juice of 1 orange

¾ cup brandy

2 splashes Angostura bitters

packed ¾ cup dark brown sugar

1⅓ cups self-rising flour

½ tsp. ground cinnamon

½ tsp. freshly grated nutmeg

½ tsp. ground cloves

4 large eggs, beaten

1 Heat the oven to 300°F (250°F
  convection oven). Grease an 8in.
  (20cm) deep, round cake pan and
  line the bottom and side with
  parchment paper.

2 Put all the dried fruit into a very
  large pan and add the ginger, 1 tbsp.
  reserved ginger syrup, the orange
  zest and juice, brandy, and Angostura
  bitters. Bring to a boil, then reduce the
  heat and simmer for 5 minutes. Add the
  butter and brown sugar and heat slowly
  to melt. Stir until the sugar dissolves.
  Take the pan off the heat and leave
  to cool for a couple of minutes.

3 Add the flour, spices, and beaten eggs,
  and mix well. Pour the batter into the
  prepared pan and smooth the surface.
  Wrap the outside of the pan in brown
  paper (a grocery-store bag is ideal) and
  secure with string to protect the cake
  during baking. Bake for 2–2½ hours—
  cover with parchment or waxed paper
  after about 1½ hours—until a skewer
  inserted into the middle comes out

clean and the cake is firm.

4 Cool in the pan for 2–3 hours, then remove from the pan, leaving the parchment paper on, transfer to a wire rack, and leave to cool completely. Wrap the cake in a layer of plastic wrap, then in foil.

Cuts into 16 slices

Calorie Gallery

140 cal ♥ 1g protein
11g fat (7g sat) ♥ 2g fiber
10g carb ♥ 0.2g salt

8

290 cal ♥ 3g protein
25g fat (4g sat) ♥ 3g fiber
15g carb 0.2g salt

10

438 cal ♥ 11g protein
21g fat (13g sat) ♥ 4g fiber
45g carb ♥ 1.3g salt

12

117 cal ♥ 3g protein
6g fat (4g sat) ♥ 4g fiber
13g carb ♥ 0.1g salt

14

280 cal ♥ 10g protein
10g fat (1g sat) ♥ 7g fiber
34g carb ♥ 1.3g salt

26

296 cal ♥ 20g protein
5g fat (1g sat) ♥ 9g fiber
47g carb ♥ 0.1g salt

28

262 cal ♥ 7g protein
7g fat (1g sat) ♥ 8g fiber
44g carb ♥ 1.3g salt

30

Per 125g (4oz) serving
(with stuffing): 301 cal
21g protein ♥ 19g fat (9g sat)
1g fiber ♥ 12g carb ♥ 0.9g salt

50

Per 125g (4oz) serving:
286 cal ♥ 21g protein
11g fat (5g sat) ♥ 1g fiber
28g carb ♥ 0.6g salt

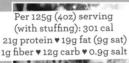

54

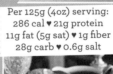

620 cal ♥ 62g protein
21g fat (6g sat) ♥ 4g fiber
24g carb ♥ 1.7g salt

66

For 8: 550 cal ♥ 55g protein
19g fat (6g sat) ♥ 2g fiber
48g carb ♥ 5.5g salt
For 10: 440 cal ♥ 44g protein
15g fat (5g sat) ♥ 2g fiber
38g carb ♥ 4.4g salt

80

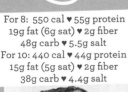

406 cals ♥ 49g protein
21g fat (7g sat) ♥ 0.3g
fiber ♥ 4g carb ♥ 6.3g salt

82

592 cal ♥ 54g protein
18g fat (7g sat) ♥ 2g fiber
56g carb ♥ 1g salt

84

645 cal ♥ 54g protein
51g fat (18g sat) ♥ 0g fiber
0g carb ♥ 0.5g salt

88

400 cal ♥ 27g protein
10g fat (5g sat) ♥ 6g fiber
53g carb ♥ 1.5g salt

3

80 cal ♥ 0.5g protein
7g fat (5g sat) ♥ 0.9 g fiber
3g carb ♥ 0.1g salt

20

50 cal ♥ 0.6g protein
trace fat ♥ 1g fiber
11g carb ♥ 0g salt

22

150 cal ♥ 4g protein
9g fat (1g sat) ♥ 4g fiber
15g carb ♥ 0.1g salt

24

506 cal ♥ 30g protein
28g fat (9g sat) ♥ 1g fiber
10g carb ♥ 1g salt

8

740 cal ♥ 49g protein
44g fat (17g sat) ♥ 3g fiber
26g carb ♥ 1.8g salt

40

854 cal ♥ 58g protein
45g fat (14g sat) ♥ 5g fiber
55g carb ♥ 3g salt

42

332 cal ♥ 29g protein
21g fat (6g sat) ♥ 0.8g fiber
6g carb ♥ 1.3g salt

46

646 cal ♥ 45g protein
41g fat (12g sat) ♥ 2g fiber
11g carb ♥ 1g salt

8

650 cal ♥ 25g protein
33g fat (13g sat) ♥ 2g fiber
65g carb ♥ 1.1g salt

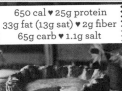

72

617 cals ♥ 31g protein
37g fat (14g sats) 2g fiber
45g carbs ♥ 2g salt

74

348 cal ♥ 28g protein
14g fat (3g sat) ♥ 8g fiber
27g carb ♥ 1.5g salt

76

662 cal ♥ 62g protein
41g fat (19g sat) ♥ 0.2g fiber
3g carb 1.4g salt

2

490 cal ♥ 39g protein
22g fat (9g sat) ♥ 2g fiber
32g carb ♥ 0.8g salt

94

536 cal ♥ 51g protein
28g fat (12g sat) ♥ 2g fiber
14g carb ♥ 1.2g salt

96

530 cal ♥ 30g protein
33g fat (20g sat) ♥ 4g fiber
27g carb ♥ 0.5g salt

98

100

102

104

108

Calorie Gallery

120

122

124

140

142

144

154

158

160

162

322 cal ♥ 57g protein
8g fat (3g sat) ♥ 0g fiber
4g carb ♥ 0.5g salt

0

382 cal ♥ 37g protein
18g fat (6g sat) ♥ 9g fiber
29g carb ♥ 1.2g salt

114

355 cal ♥ 30g protein
16g fat (6g sat) ♥ 4g fiber
23g carb ♥ 1.2g salt

116

474 cal ♥ 39g protein
27g fat (11g sat) ♥ 2g fiber
11g carb ♥ 0.7g salt

118

1036 cal ♥ 55g protein
57g fat (10g sat) ♥ 1g fiber
65g carb ♥ 1.4g salt

6

Without lime butter: 184 cal
4g protein ♥ 8g fat (1g sat)
4g fiber ♥ 21g carb ♥ 1.3g salt

134

173 cal ♥ 8g protein
2g fat (trace sat) ♥ 4g fiber
35g carb ♥ 2.3g salt

136

323 cal ♥ 31g protein
18g fat (5g sat) ♥ 3g fiber
17g carb ♥ 0.9g salt

138

408 cal ♥ 29g protein
19g fat (7g sat) ♥ 6g fiber
28g carb ♥ 1.1g salt

6

586 cal ♥ 52g protein
29g fat (10g sat) ♥ 3g fiber
31 carb ♥ 0.4g salt

150

478 cal ♥ 32g protein
28g fat (16g sat) ♥ 2g fiber
12g carb ♥ 0.7g salt

152

517 cal ♥ 46g protein
30g fat (116 sat) ♥ 2g fiber
16g carb ♥ 1.6g salt

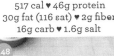

148

139 cal ♥ 1g protein
trace fat ♥ 3g fiber
26g carb ♥ 0.1g salt

4

448 cal ♥ 5g protein
17g fat (7g sat) ♥ 2g fiber
68g carb ♥ 0.3g salt

166

Per slice: 384 cal
5g protein ♥ 11g fat (6g sat)
2g fiber ♥ 71g carb ♥ 0.2g salt

168

Index

PICTURE CREDITS

Photographers: Neil Barclay
(pages 39 and 127); Martin
Brigdale (page 161); Nicki Dowey
(pages 9, 11, 13, 17, 21, 23, 25, 27,
29, 41, 67, 69, 77, 81, 93, 97, 101, 115,
119, 121, 125, 135, 139, 141, 145, 147,
149, 153, 155,163, 165, 167 and 169);
Fiona Kennedy (pages 43, 75, 112
and 123); Gareth Morgans
(pages 47, 51, 52, 53, 55 and 111);
Myles New (page 151); Craig
Robertson (pages 15, 18, 19, 31, 34,
35, 36, 45, 60, 61, 64, 65, 78, 79, 85,
87, 99, 105, 107, 109, 113, 137, 143
and 159); Maja Smend (pages 73
and 95); Lucinda Symons (pages
83, 103 and 117); Kate Whitaker
(page 89) Rachel Whiting
(front cover).

Home Economists:
Anna Burges-Lumsden,
Joanna Farrow, Emma Jane Frost,
Teresa Goldfinch, Alice Hart,
Lucy McKelvie, Kim Morphew,
Aya Nishimura, Katie Rogers,
Bridget Sargeson, Sarah Tildesley,
Kate Trend, Jennifer White and
Mari Mererid Williams.

Stylists:
Susannah Blake, Tamzin
Ferdinando, Wei Tang,
Sarah Tildesley, Helen Trent and
Fanny Ward.

CHEAP EATS

Budget-Busting Ideas That Won't Break the Bank

FLASH *in the* **PAN**

Spice Up Your Noodles & Stir-Fries

LET'S *do* **BRUNCH**

Mouth-Watering Meals to Start Your Day

PARTY FOOD

Delicious Recipes to Get the Party Started

ROAST IT

There's Nothing Better Than a Delicious Roast

SLOW COOK IT

Slow-Cooked Meals Packed with Flavor